Literature in Education:
Encounter and Experience

Edwin Webb

 The Falmer Press

(A Member of the Taylor & Francis Group)
London • New York • Philadelphia

UK   The Falmer Press, 4 John Street, London WC1N 2ET
USA   The Falmer Press, Taylor & Francis Inc., 1900 Frost Road, Suite 101, Bristol, PA 19007

© Edwin Webb 1992

First published 1992

The author and publishers thank the following for permission to quote from copyright material: Dannie Abse and Hutchinson and Co Ltd for the extract from 'Duality' from *Tenants of the House*; the estate of Thomas Blackburn and Hutchinson and Co Ltd for 'Hospital for Defectives' from *Selected Poems*; Melvyn Bragg and Hodder and Stoughton Ltd for the passage from *The Maid of Buttermere*; Mrs Valerie Eliot and Messrs Faber and Faber Ltd for lines from 'The Love Song of J. Alfred Prufrock' and 'Journey of the Magi' (*Collected Poems 1909–1962*), and for extracts from 'Tradition and the Individual Talent' (*Selected Essays 1917–1932*), *The Use of Poetry and the Use of Criticism*, and *On Poetry and Poets*; for extracts from 'Notes on an Unfinished Novel' (c) John Fowles (1969) to the author and Fontana/Collins; William Golding and Messrs Faber and Faber Ltd for a passage from 'Fable' in *The Hot Gates*; Louis J. Halle and Chatto and Windus for the extract from *The Society of Man*; James MacGibbon and Penguin Books Ltd for Stevie Smith's 'Not Waving But Drowning' from *The Collected Poems of Stevie Smith*.

A catalogue record for this book is available from the British Library

ISBN 1 85000 767 5
ISBN 1 85000 768 3 (pbk)

Library of Congress Cataloging-in-Publication Data available on request

Jacket design by Benedict Evans

Typeset in 10/11pt Bembo by
Graphicraft Typesetters Ltd., Hong Kong

Printed in Great Britain by Burgess Science Press, Basingstoke on paper which has a specified pH value on final paper manufacture of not less than 7.5 and is therefore 'acid free'.

Literature in Education

The Falmer Press Library on Aesthetic Education

Series Editor: Dr Peter Abbs, University of Sussex, UK

Setting the Frame

LIVING POWERS:
The Arts in Education
Edited by Peter Abbs

A IS FOR AESTHETIC:
Essays on Creative and
Aesthetic Education
Peter Abbs

THE SYMBOLIC ORDER:
A Contemporary Reader on the
Arts Debate
Edited by Peter Abbs

THE RATIONALITY OF
FEELING:
Understanding the Arts in Education
David Best

The Individual Studies

FILM AND TELEVISION IN
EDUCATION:
An Aesthetic Approach to the
Moving Image
Robert Watson

LITERATURE IN
EDUCATION:
Encounter and Experience
Edwin Webb

DANCE AS EDUCATION:
Towards a National Dance Culture
Peter Brinson

THE VISUAL ARTS IN
EDUCATION
Rod Taylor

MUSIC EDUCATION IN
THEORY AND PRACTICE
Charles Plummeridge

THE ARTS IN THE PRIMARY
SCHOOL
Glennis Andrews and Rod Taylor

EDUCATION IN DRAMA:
Casting the Dramatic Curriculum
David Hornbrook

Work of Reference

KEY CONCEPTS:
A Guide to Aesthetics, Criticism and the Arts in Education
Trevor Pateman

Contents

Acknowledgments

I should like to record my grateful thanks to Peter Abbs on two counts: first, as Series Editor of the Falmer Press Library on Aesthetic Education, for inviting me to undertake the writing of this book; and second, for his restrained but perceptive comments on the copy. The final version owes a good deal, therefore, to his gentle persuasiveness. I must thank Falmer Press, too, for offering me an extended completion-time in order that I could undertake the book, knowing that I had prior commitments to other projects.

The Dedication of this book to Edward Lee and Felix Cross enables me to fulfil a private ambition in this recognition of the excitements and challenges of working with them in concert and in recording studio — and for all which I have learned as a consequence. I owe an additional debt of gratitude to Edward Lee who over the years has helped me to refine and make more explicit my own practices and beliefs, and for his unerring ability to pose the awkward, unignorably pertinent, question. His comments on drafts of sections of this work enabled me to redesign the structure of the book. I must also thank Pat Barrett and Tom Ralph for their reading of parts of the text, and for their helpful comments.

I am particularly indebted to Carol Saumarez not only for her scrupulous copy-editing of the entire text, but also for those many occasions when her challenges and suggestions have led to distinct improvements in expression and clarity. The book is certainly the better for her critical reading of the whole.

Whatever there may be of merit in this book is owed to my students, young and mature, in schools, colleges of Further Education, Universities and Polytechnics, with whom I have shared in explorations of the literary experience. It is these explorations which now are offered to other audiences.

Edwin Webb
October 1990

Series Editor's Preface

To understand the radical nature of Edwin Webb's *Literature in Education* it is necessary to consider the traditional placing of literature in the curriculum. For the best part of a century literature, first developing out of the study of the classics and then largely replacing them, was classified as one of the Humanities and not one of the Arts. In the Hadow Report of 1927, for example, one finds Literature linked to Language, Foreign Languages and History. In the Spens Report it is listed with English, Religious Education (Scripture), History and Geography. Again, in the Newsom Report of 1963, it is squarely placed in the chapter headed 'The Humanities' while Dance, Art and Music are found in a separate chapter entitled 'The Practical Subjects'. This isolation of Literature from the Arts has been so strong that many have come to see it is an irreducible part of the order of things. It has been little reflected on and seldom questioned. And yet while securing literature an important place in the curriculum, it has simultaneously cut it off from its artistic partners and somewhat distorted its intrinsic identity.

Furthermore, we are now able to see that the preoccupation with social issues and social themes which came to characterize the teaching of literature in most comprehensive schools throughout the 60s and 70s was the all but inevitable outcome of a 'Humanities Logic'. If History is seen as an analogous discipline (and not, say, Music or Art) then it is not surprising that social issues are envisaged as the integrating concern of literature teaching. Indeed, for the best part of three decades, contemporary issues and the social experience of the child came to usurp the whole inherited field of literature. In 1972 Leslie Stratta, the co-author of a popular English course book *Reflections* (which in the course of two years work only offered one complete poem to its adolescent readers) wrote:

> Twenty years ago a teacher of English might have confidently asserted that his main concern was to introduce his pupils to literature. Today he might less confidently assert that his main concern is with the process of helping his pupils to develop their abilities in *using language for a variety of needs and purposes*... But part of this change results from the realisation *that using literature almost exclusively is too abstract an approach* for many pupils, which rather than engage their interests, may well prove to be a barrier...[1] (my italics)

Having placed Literature at the edge of the teaching programme, Stratta continued:

> Reading, especially of literature, presents all pupils with a number of problems. Books are *frequently long or longish, the language used, especially of poetry, is often dense and difficult,* more so if the work is from the heritage, the vision of life presented comes from the mature imagination of an adult mind.[2] (my italics)

It is not the place to examine the extraordinary assumptions which inform these philistine paragraphs, but it is important to notice the extreme nature of the crisis it records. Even the Bullock Report (1975) which, in its turn, only offered fifteen out of its 609 pages on the value of literature, noted with concern that 'we have a definite impression that fewer full length novels are read',[3] and urged that, where anthologies were used, they should 'include complete pieces or substantial extracts, artistic units on their own, rather than merely snippets clipped out of their contexts'.[4] It is around this period that we can date the disappearance of the literary field from the average comprehensive classroom and the onset of a frightening cultural amnesia from which as a nation we have still to recover.

Of course, the reader will be right, at this point, to protest, to point out that there were other voices in the tradition of English teaching: the distant but living voices of Coleridge and Arnold, the not so distant voices of George Sampson and F.R. Leavis, the more recent voices of Marjorie Hourd and David Holbrook. It is true that their work struggled to make literature and the related development of sensibility central. And it is here that we arrive at a good position to see the importance of this present study; for what this book intends to do is to reclaim literature *as literature* (against all those who would use it as poor sociology, or now as 'communications') by *taking much of the prior literary tradition evoked above out of the matrix of the Humanities and into that of the Arts.* Thus, what is offered to the reader is a distinctively artistic and aesthetic approach to the teaching of literature; a poetics of the creative act and the imaginative work of art.

In an earlier volume of the Aesthetic Library, *The Symbolic Order,* George Whalley argued that in the teaching of literature 'the first lesson is to engage the senses, not as an agreeable adjunct to other more intellectual delights, but as the necessary means to hold the mind in the perceptual mode, to keep the habits of abstraction and generalization in their place'.[5] This is, precisely, the approach developed by Edwin Webb. Again and again, he delineates the aesthetic nature of literary creation and response and moves on to examine its implications for the teaching of literature. He shows us the kinaesthetic images informing the poetic language of 'Leda and the Swan': he suggests how in the teaching of William Blake's 'The Sick Rose' teachers can prefigure the *gestalt* of that poem through prior work in free association; he illustrates the power and place of the oral rendering of written texts. His philosophy of symbolic making and his actual method of teaching flow in and out of each other, are part of that single act of understanding which is built on the premise *first apprehension, then comprehension* or, perhaps even better, *comprehension through apprehension!*

One of the key terms in the Aesthetic Education Library is aesthetic field. It is a term much invoked in the pages that follow. It denotes first the various sequential phases in the creation of art, from the act of *making* to the *presenting* of the realized work, through to the audience's *responding* and the complex *evaluation* of the art (a process described much more adequately in the first chapter of *Living Powers: The Arts in Education*). The second meaning refers to the symbolic system within which the work is made, performed, responded to and evaluated. In *Literature in Education* both meanings are systematically explored. In Parts II and III Edwin Webb adapts and extends the model of the aesthetic field for the teaching of literature; while in the more theoretical Part I, he elaborates on the notion of the symbolic system, positing the notion of *genre* as a valuable category for the structuring of the teaching of literature. Here, however, he takes issue with those Structuralists who would see the system as somehow self-sustaining and, as it were, an end in itself. Rightly, he insists that it is the creative individual who activates the system and who, in turn, is developed by the interaction. In this context he quotes Denis Donoghue's remark: 'A linguistic system makes certain things possible, but makes nothing actual'.[6] It is the individual who actualizes and it is the individual who is educated in the process. The subtitle of the study is *Encounter and Experience*. At the heart of the imaginative and aesthetic enterprise lies the education of the psyche.

Here then is a poetics for the teaching of literature as one of the six great arts. However, having emphasized its radical nature, its departure from much recent practice, I must now stress that there is no reason why, as a method, it should not be implemented in any classroom in the present educational system. In the book Edwin Webb himself takes a number of recent GCSE demands which are framed within an artistic conception of literature. Furthermore, there are a number of 'A' level syllabuses which invite and evaluate that subtle interactive mixture of expressive and evaluative work which is proposed here. Perhaps even more important, the 1989 DES document, *National Curriculum Proposals for English for ages 5 to 16* (The Cox Report) declared:

> Literature has an important role to play — in a variety of ways — in improving abilities in speaking and listening and in writing, as well as in reading. Children should experiment, for example, with dramatic improvisations of the stories they read and write; they should experience and take part in the performance of poetry; they should listen critically to radio plays. They should also be encouraged to write fiction, poetry, plays, diaries, book reviews and so on, in response to the literature they have enjoyed and shared and discussed with their teacher and classmates. Learning to read and learning to write are intimately related. By reading a wide range of literature, children become aware of new forms of discourse and modes of expression with which they may experiment in their own writing.[7]

This is precisely the approach of Edwin Webb; the only difference is that unlike the Cox Report, Edwin Webb provides a profound educational philosophy to justify and illuminate the method. It is a philosophy which accords with that of the Aesthetic Library and in the present utilitarian time is one very much needed, not only within the teaching of literature, but within the Arts and society at large.

Peter Abbs
Centre for Language, Literature and the Arts in Education
University of Sussex
October 1990

Notes and References

1 Stratta, L. (1972) 'Language and experience: thoughts on a rationale for the teaching of English', *English in Education*, **6**, no. 3, p. 98 and p. 100.
2 *Ibid.*, p. 108.
3 (1975) *A Language for Life*, HMSO, p. 132.
4 *Ibid.*
5 Whalley, G. (1989) 'Teaching Poetry' in Abbs, P. (Ed.) *The Symbolic Order: A Contemporary Reader on the Arts Debate*, London, Falmer Press, pp. 227–8.
6 Donoghue, D. (1989) 'The Domestication of Outrage' in Abbs, P. (Ed.) *The Symbolic Order: A Contemporary Reader on the Arts Debate*, London, Falmer Press, p. 111.
7 (1989) *English for Ages 5 to 16*, DES, ch. 7, para. 7.8.

Introduction

The history of English teaching, as I have previously characterized it, may be seen as a continuing clash between 'content' and 'process', and between those philosophies which propose a 'literary' conception of English against that of a 'language' concern. The resultant confusions between these conceptions and the consequent fall-out of competing aims, objectives, and procedures, still typify much of the educational debate for the teaching of English. The uncertainty is compounded by those who would view English as a branch of social studies, or media studies, or communications. In many educational contexts the centrality of literature has been squeezed out.

In the secondary and tertiary sectors of education, it is often held that the business of English teaching should devote itself to a functional operationalism: the promotion of language 'skills'. This view of the responsibility of the English teacher to the student is sometimes expressed in specific and elaborate attainment criteria — and on many other occasions the slogan 'spelling, punctuation, and grammar' is used to convey the looser sentiment as to what the job of the English teacher should *really* be concerned with (or, as to that with which the job should be concerned really). At the time of writing the debate has taken another turn, issuing in the demand, within the requirements of the National Curriculum, that school students should develop explicit knowledge *of* language. As recommended in the Cox Report (*National Curriculum Proposals for English for Ages 5 to 16*, June 1989), these projections of language study were challenged by the majority of respondents to this document in the National Curriculum Council Consultation Report (November 1989) for its 'overemphasis on the functional aspects of language at the expense of the personal and imaginative'. The demand that 'knowledge about language' should guide, or bind, the teaching of English follows the sociolinguistic line of development which one can trace back to the middle 1960s and through the Bullock Report, *A Language for Life* (1975). Since I have outlined these matters elsewhere, I shall not repeat them here.[1]

Whilst acknowledging that students should experience, and become competent in dealing with, a wide and diverse range of language forms, it is important to recognize this simple fact: that knowledge *about* language will not necessarily make students more able to *use* language in either written or spoken mode, in relation to any identified audience, in any particular situation, context, register, dialect, style, tone. Or in any of those other descriptives of language which we can extrapolate from any given usage. Were this so, we would expect to find the most felicitous and perfected use of language in the writings of the linguisticians themselves! For who knows more *about* language than they? The reality, for all of us who have studied linguistics is, I submit, an experience of a very different order.

There is a corollary truth to this demand for rigour, as it is sometimes expressed, in the students' study of language. And it is that *what they are to know about language they already do know*. It is implicitly known; it is known in the act of utterance itself. Grammar is an invention of grammarians. One does not speak grammar, nor does one need that knowledge, which grammarians call grammar, in order to speak. One speaks a language which, in the case of first language acquisition, and despite the lack of any formal knowledge of the linguisticians' abstractions of language, *makes sense* — as it did before grammarians were invented. For it is that prime function of making sense to which all other uses of language refer. Our students know this too, as they certainly know when something does *not* make sense.

In an article by members of the Language in the National Curriculum Project, who are active supporters of the move towards the teaching of explicit knowledge of language, the same admission is made — though it seems to have gone unrecognized that the very case proposed has thereby been forfeited in large measure. In a passage of more than two hundred words of the full copy they detail 'What pupils already know about language'. Too lengthy to quote in its entirety, the passage begins:

> Pupils' knowledge about language is frequently ignored or underestimated. Their competence as language users depends on a creative use of implicit grammatical knowledge, arguably innate, together with acquired knowledge about social structures and functions encoded in language... They know, for example, about word order in English sentences...[2]

There follows a list of at least another thirty-seven things which, it is asserted, the pupils already know. So: if they do know these matters already, why on earth should we expend great effort and time to teach them these things? So that they can spot and label correctly the modal verb and get a big tick for so doing? The real challenge is not to teach students what they already know, but to *use* what they know so that they may explore what they do *not* know. That is what education is, from *educere*, to lead out.

The exploration which literature and the arts proposes is the imaginative journey into one's own world of experience and the worlds of experience of others. It too, will use the students' implicit knowledge of language, and will develop their understanding of what language is and what language does, but in relation to establishing further understandings of experience. Language, in this exploration, regains its prime and mysterious symbolic purpose: it becomes the *means* by which we focus our consciousness, not the focus itself. And in that reflexivity of consciousness which language makes possible, we make and discover self-consciousness. In that exploration we discover our realities, and a sense of identity, of self and that of others. For literature extends the possibility of experience within the shared and the communal. The creative making of literature assists us to come into possession of our selves, to construct a sense of meaning — to further the movement into self-realization and the understanding of others. The reading of literature is an extension of self through the re-creation of meaning — oneself in relation to the text and the responses of others. Literature is not a decorative or precious acquisition; nor is it a body of knowledge. It is a fundamental pursuit of the human endeavour to come to know the reality of experience, and in so doing, to vivify our living within an enlarging sense of being. These, which it is the business of this book to elaborate, are some of the fundamental propositions which will argue for the centrality of the literary experience within the English programme. From Matthew Arnold, through Caldwell Cook and George Sampson, F.R. Leavis, Marjorie Hourd, David Holbrook, and others (all with their own individual contributions to the enterprise) descends this insistent tradition; a tradition which stresses the absolute and vital need for the direct and creative experience of language, and for engagement with those realms of experience which literary forms symbolize.

*

Many teachers are torn between beliefs such as these and the demands imposed upon them to teach language, or knowledge about language. Some of this indecisiveness can show itself not simply in the veering of the debate, but perhaps in even clearer outline through some of the practices adopted by some teachers. Let me illustrate the dilemma with an actual example. I have before me a worksheet, prepared by a teacher of some years' standing, which cogently illustrates the uncertainties I am pointing to, both of conception and of method. I reproduce the worksheet in its entirety:

NOT WAVING BUT DROWNING   WORKSHEET

> Nobody heard him, the dead man,
> But still he lay moaning:
> I was much further out than you thought
> And not waving but drowning.
>
> Poor chap, he always loved larking
> And now he's dead
> It must have been too cold for him his heart gave way
> They said.
>
> Oh, no no no, it was too cold always
> (Still the dead one lay moaning)
> I was much too far out all my life
> And not waving but drowning.

Stevie Smith

Answer the following questions as fully as you can in your own words, in sentences.

1. What two possible reasons could there be for no-one hearing the man as he moaned?   2
2. He was 'not waving but drowning'.
   (a) What signal did the man make?   1
   (b) How was the signal interpreted?   1
   (c) What had he intended to convey by his signal?   1
3. What two possible reasons could there be for the misinterpretation of the signal?   2
4. What reason is suggested for his death?   1
5. The man though he is still moaning is called 'the dead man'. Suggest a reason for this.   1
6. Re-read the last verse.
   Apart from the sea water being cold, from swimming out of his depth, what could the
   man be suggesting about himself, his life and other people and their reactions by his
   comments?   3

Total: 12

Extra

From your reading of the section 'Technical Gestures' (*Manwatching*) *suggest* the signal the
man should have used to illustrate his predicament.

Discuss the man's predicament with particular reference to Question 6.

Write a short story entitled

   'If only I had known ...'

   or

Write a personal response essay about an experience or a situation which has made you feel
'if only I had known'. Explain how your behaviour would have been different. Suggest what
you have learned from this experience.

I invite the reader to answer the questions, as set. I shall then not need to
make detailed comment on the silliness of some of the questions, but be able
to reserve space for comment of a larger order.

For once again we see a literary work, and a very fine one in the case of
this poem, subverted to a different order of expression, translated into and
treated with a literalness of composition. The nature of the literary embodiment of meaning or significance is ignored. Even the essential ambiguities of

the poem — which I am sure most teachers would wish to *talk through* with their pupils — are seized upon as providing opportunities for a comprehension test. Sadly, many pupils know very well that literature, and poetry in particular, is just that: a comprehension test. Where William Empson, as literary critic, claimed that the 'puzzle interest' of a poem is one of its attractions, there are many pupils, and older students alike, who 'just don't see what it means'.

As in the worksheet above, so in a good deal of what passes for literature teaching, there is no attempt to engage with the experience projected by the poem. Question 6, in the example above, identifies the area of engagement; what might be discussed as an experience of living. But as set, the question can not be answered since we, the readers, know nothing about the man's biographical details. The poem does not tell us about 'his life and other people and their reactions'; it informs us, if we will listen to the poem, about his *condition*. The connection to that is made out of the reader's experience of living. At one level this might be a simple identification; something in one's own autobiographical experience which matches the literary, personal associations suggested out of the context of the poem. Another response may enable us to see the poem, to recognize its implications, as an experience in which we all share, to lesser, to greater, degree. The poem is its own metaphor: its procedures are not those of the telephone directory, and its challenge is not one of information-retrieval.

In the context of Higher Education, response to literature can sometimes appear to be no more than a special kind of language-game. Here, for example, students' experience of literature is directed to opportunities for study which concern themselves with the identification and deconstruction of ideologies, overt or implied — but especially political and sexual — within the literary *texte*. The very use of the term *texte*, which has come to stand now for almost any cultural or artistic product or phenomenon, can itself take us away from that which is specifically literary; so that what is special to the literary *experience* of poems, novels and other literary forms as *art*, may thereby be diminished or even ignored. Such engagements with *texte*, the de-construction (to destruction) of those signs composing the original, are then played out in elaborate language-moves upon the verbal specimen, the literary work. The language of a literary work is first, however, a symbol directing us elsewhere. That elsewhere is not the surface of the paper, nor indeed solely the lexicon of ideological ideas by which we can rewrite the *texte*, testing it to destruction, but a challenge to us creatively to *reconstruct*, in cooperation with the work, that potential of human experience from which it originated. That is the *literary experience* to be explored; not the fact of the language, but what the language points us towards. It is to *that* re-creation which the art work invites us to respond. To do that, of course, demands that we engage with language intensively and creatively; but in ways which, alas, the facility to name the parts of speech of the language will assist not one jot.

There is no feature of our living which literature fails to touch, and it is in touch and touching, the most intimate of all sensate experience, that reside some important clues as to the nature of the literary experience. Both to create, in our own writings, and to re-create, in our reading, the literary experience we need to be in touch with those psychic processes which language nominates and construes through its symbolizations. Most vitally, the experience of literature — just as that experience from which it is shaped — will induce responses of feeling. Feeling is a fundamental means by which we keep in touch with ourselves and, therefore, others. Simultaneously as it involves our feeling, the literary experience will invite direct and immediate sensuous responses. Such sensuous apprehension is both perceptual and affective; and in this complex of response there is knowing too, an element of cognition — in our disposition towards the literary experience and what, thereby, we see and come to understand. All of this is implied in the use of the term *aesthetic* which, again, it is the business of this book to attempt to delineate. As we come to know, both in the making of literary forms and in the re-creative act of their reading, so we may move to more considered and reflective judgment upon the particularities of the literary experience. Such evaluations of experience will be arrived at through intellectual operations of thought, our capacities for abstracting and generalizing, and the expression of our thought in discussion and reason. Thus both apprehension and comprehension are involved in the aesthetic domain, and the literary experience induces responses both of sensibility and sense.

Whatever other forms of language use the English teacher will help students to develop, none is more important than that of the literary-expressive discipline of making and remaking in the aesthetic mode. Within the English programme in secondary schools, therefore, this book argues for the centrality of the experience of literature as art: of literature as a vital imaginative mode for the apprehension of our realities. It is a view of the literary enterprise intended also to inform the manner in which literary programmes may be offered within Higher Education contexts which, in the main, fail to explore the aesthetic field of literature.

Literature, in the terms of reference given for the composition of this book, excluded drama. It will be quite evident in what follows, however, that the exploration of the aesthetic field of literature (poetry, story, and other genres) connects vitally and of necessity with dramatic forms of literature. For drama is not only a form of literature in its own right, it is a *mode* by which *the enactment of meaning* is presented. Thus in discussing notions of presentation, performance, and creative transposition, for example, connections have been made with the dramatic activities of art-making. Through these natural extensions of the literary into the dramatic, there are suggestions for associations with other arts within a community of expressive activities.

Literary works of the imagination synthesize within the individuality of each discrete form the *fullness* of each experience which they present. Imagination enables us to connect with experience in ways simply not available to us in the moment or duration of experiencing itself. Imagination is, from the beginning, a reflective cast upon experience. This is why, as Thornton Wilder expressed it in *The Ides of March* (1948), 'The poets are the true prophets.' Not the poets only, but creative writers in all forms, and makers across all the arts are the prophets of a society. Some, in a very narrow use of the word, are tellers of the future; but *all* authentic art reconstitutes the present condition so that we may recognize it, and in that recognition, know again what can be overlooked. For in that telling, as in the example of the Old Testament prophets, we see more clearly as individuals and as societies what that condition is. The function of art thereby, and of necessity, engages a moral sense. To fail to apprehend the present is to doom ourselves to unconscious being and an unthought future.

Notes and References

1 'English as Aesthetic Initiative', in Abbs, P. (Ed.) (1987), *Living Powers*, London, Falmer Press.
2 'Learning Not To Sneer' (1990) *Times Educational Supplement*, November 5. A trenchant counter, by Roger Knight, to this article is carried in the same issue of the *TES* ('Hollow at the Core?').

Part I

Literature and the Reality of Experience: Dimensions of Encounter

In the creative encounter with the world of experience, the questings of consciousness explore its realities and seek to give shape to their discoveries. Such an impulse to create begins in the desire to make sense of experience. In this exploration of the present, memory — that which is subliminally-held, as well as that which is securely known — is engaged; and its connections and associations shaped through the agency of imagination in the literary work. The making of the art construes meaning, conferring order upon experience; shaping in the act of discovery, and discovering in the act of making. In the impulse to create, there is encounter with the need for form — without which the reality of experience itself would subsist without definition. The making of the particular form of the piece connects with other examples of form and genres: traditions of disposing of the symbols of that art within a culture or cultures. Mediating and negotiating all of these dimensions of the literary encounter is the medium of language itself: the means of symbolization through which experience may be transformed into expressive realization.

Chapter 1

Encounter and Experience

What has fascinated me all my life is
the way people make their world
intelligible.

Roland Barthes[1]

The Reality of Experience

At the centre of the creative enterprise there is encounter. It is the encounter
of consciousness with the reality of experience. Experience includes, of
course, what we think of as the objective world which is 'out there', but the
reality of experience is that which identifies and defines one's self in relation
to that phenomenal world. Similarly, experience includes all that we think of
as subjective — the promptings and urgings of the psyche. But the reality of
an individual's world is fashioned by the manner in which the conscious
individual responds to experience, and in those responses begins to shape,
understand, and come to terms with experience.

The reality of experience constituting the individual's world thus implies
that network of relationships by which one identifies one's self, the 'inner'
life of one's own psyche, and one's self in relation to the phenomenal world
and the worlds of others. The reality of experience is what one makes, or has
made, of the living experience. For this world of individual reality, compounded of experience, direct and indirect, carries with it an impulse towards
meaning and the urge to make sense of one's living. The reality of experience
moves towards both self-realization and individuation — a coming to know
'self' in relation to the physical world and the worlds of others.

The reality of experience is a creative formulation. Reality is not given.
It is shaped. Such realities may be knowingly held, or impulsively acted out
— action prompted out of unconscious personality, from which the reality
may be subsequently deduced. But realities of experience do not make
themselves. One may, for example, have a flashing insight. The insight may
appear to be quite involuntary. But if that insight is to find its location within
the reality of experience, it must, at the very least, be *attended to* — and

reflected upon: it must be related to other conditions or forms of experience for its pertinence (its reality) to be realized.

The creative encounter with the reality of experience can itself result in many forms: reflection, exposition, the design of theory, for example. A creative encounter may also be artistic; it leads to art-making and results in works of art. Here the encounter is manifold, and may be sequential or simultaneous — the dimensions of the encounter operating individually or severally. To the exploration of other significant features of the *artistic* encounter I shall return in succeeding chapters. What is important to note here is that where the encounter results in an art product, there is also a shaping of reality: and the art becomes *a means towards meaning*. That means towards meaning will in part be consequent upon the particular art form: whether literature, drama, dance, film, music, or the visual arts — all of which employ distinctive modes of experience, and ways of experiencing, as their shaping materials. The advantage, which all these modes of art share, is that through their symbolic forms of presentation the encounter with experience may be more inclusively expressed; the reality of experience reconstituted, so that it may be understood in ways which the partiality of rational discourse ignores, because of the inherent laws of its own procedures of operation. Reason itself, almost invariably, will be involved in the art-making process, at the time of making and subsequently. Indeed, one of the most vital of all justifying arguments for our fundamental need of art is precisely that it does promote an extension of our reasoning and explicit understanding. But reason alone can not *generate* the art.

The world of experience and the reality of experience are not synonymous. The world of experience, potentially, is all that the individual has witnessed or undergone — the events and occurrences of one's living. It has a past tense, which is memory. But the world of experience is also immediate; a present which may confirm, challenge, reorder the past. Reality is experience endowed with significance. Experience and its reality may confront each other, the established reality influencing the present experience, the present experience reviewing, and then perhaps modifying notions of reality derived from past experience.

The world of experience includes that which is known and acknowledged in the form of thought, idea, and belief, together with those data and perceptions which have informed and shaped such thoughts, ideas and beliefs. Thus the world of experience also includes that which is unknown, subliminally or unconsciously held but revealed to consciousness in image, symbol, dream and myth. As these emerge into awareness, so may the individual consciously play over them and determine their significance as they combine and relate to each other and to other known elements of consciousness. To take one example of the creative encounter, we may cite that of dreams. Here the images, movements, and sounds of the dream unconsciously present themselves to awareness. The act of dreaming is in itself involuntary.[2] The events of the dream, however, may be recalled, and they may seem to have significance — somehow that dream *matters*. But it is the active working-over of the recollection, a conscious apprehending and questioning and relating, which will endow the dream with meaning. The conscious faculty of the personality in this encounter — to return the word to its full import — then *re-cognizes* the world of experience contained in the dream. Such recognition not only 'sees again' but *knows* again, so that we are literally reminded. The images, symbols and language of art-forms similarly may employ materials drawn from the entire range of experience. The fashioning of their arrangement, both in sequence and contiguity will develop a sense of meaning, one which will be implicatory rather than fully expressed, as in a didactic mode.

The relationship between the person and his or her world of experience is reciprocal: the living experience and the sensed reality of one's world necessarily influence each other. That is why certain events in our lives cause our world of reality to fall apart, be amended, or be enriched.

The reality of experience is not simply the biographical chronology of the individual's life. The reality of experience is the critical movement towards understanding through the attempt to reflect on that life. Understanding may be explicit — stated as belief or fully-expressed thought, or implicit — a sense of meaning woven into and through the narrative events and circumstances of a life, for the world of experience subsists at many levels of consciousness.

Consciousness and Psyche

There is that level of consciousness, which we may denote by the term *mind*, in which things are known to and may be identified positively by the person — the world of data, facts, ideas and thoughts. There is *pre-consciousness* — the world of experience in the process of becoming. There is the *personal unconscious* — elements of which may be revealed to awareness in image and symbol, endowed with private meaning or association. There is a *shared unconscious* — communal experience embodied in the form of symbol and myth of a culture. Daily our living experience contributes to this accumulation of consciousness. One cannot be aware of its totality in any given moment, of course. Much can be recalled by conscious effort, much is 'triggered' in the presence of a particular moment — the actuality in a moment of one's living. Much can be embodied in the symbolization of art-making; for the symbols of art are accretions and combinations which contrive to 'mean more than they say'.

In speaking of consciousness, though, we are condemned to the use of metaphor. The conventions of 'levels' of consciousness carry certain implications to be challenged, particularly if we are to understand the nature of the artistic encounter which transforms the world of experience into a sense of meaning. The 'basement-to-attic' model of consciousness implies a hierarchical progression in which each stage of consciousness progresses upwards finally to emerge into a state of clear awareness.

The world of experience does not operate in this way. For each region of consciousness may become *immediately* present without having to progress through intervening stages. There is overlap, interchange, and intimate connection among and between all of the regions of consciousness. Rather than a hierarchical model, what is required is a molecular conception in which the regions or nodes of consciousness may have pathways to each other *in all directions.* Certainly the artistic encounter with the world of experience (the sum-total of all individual memory held in consciousness, pre-consciousness, and unconsciousness) shows just such potential connectedness.

There is, I believe, another qualification to add. The world of experience must be seen, additionally, as something more than a mere repository of memory. It must be seen, too, as dynamic, its possessions acting upon, reacting to, and interacting with each other, within memory itself, and in reaction to the momentary experiencing of the present. Neither memory nor time stands still; the world of experience is constantly animated, shifting and adjusting, through the operation upon it of those forces of consciousness by which we both apprehend experience and shape our realities. To these forces we may subscribe the term *psyche*.

Psyche presumes much more than the agency of mind alone. For psyche takes us from mentalism back to the psycho-biology of the total person. The notion enables us to admit other functions of the psyche, each of which may have a unique claim to attention on occasion, whilst on other occasions they may operate simultaneously in a nexus of consciousness. All are powerful agencies by which we possess the world of experience.

There is, of course, *thinking* — the understanding of the world through cognition. There is *feeling* — a perception of value or significance in the world of experience, a qualitative evaluation. There is *sensing* — experience produced directly or indirectly by the sense organs, internal and external (including both immediate sensation and after-the-effect awarenesses). There is *intuiting* — the immediate and direct apprehension that something is so, 'knowing something without knowing how you know it', or a perception via the unconscious.[3]

Though tentatively offered, these descriptions refer us to crucial functionings of consciousness: *the means by which one experiences.* Through these means we apprehend experience and move towards its comprehension. Through them we are aware of what we are experiencing in any moment of our living. The evidences of experience which they provide may be ignored, or suppressed; or selection may be made among them according to what we choose to give attention to. Just as these forces of the psyche inform our present, so they may shape our past. They may operate retro-actively, as it were, upon memory. It is not uncommon, for example, not to become aware of what one *was feeling* at a given moment until after the event has passed. The recall is active, our attention is given to the elucidation of what it was we felt *then*, because somehow it is important *now*. What I am pointing to is that thinking, feeling, sensing and intuiting should be perceived as *active* processes — which is why they have here been offered in verb form. They are the means by which one actively encounters and animates the world of experience.

It is important, too, to distinguish between the operation of these means and their products: the product of thinking is a thought, the product of feeling is a feeling ... and so on. These products then may enter and be possessed in the world of experience, the 'memory-bank' of the consciousness of the individual personality. As active verbs they are intended to convey a sense of themselves as the dynamic and shaping forces which constitute experience, as well as means of responding to experience. They are the potent forces by which the world of experience is both compounded and explored, its possessions gained, and the means by which consciousness comes to awareness of self and awareness of self in relation to the phenomenal world and the world of experience of others. Thinking, feeling, sensing, and intuiting construe the world of experience. To construe the world of experience in the act of encounter, however provisionally, is to put a construction upon it — to make sense of that world.

To those means by which we acquire experience must be added another operation by which we construe that world: that abstracting and synthesizing faculty we call imagination. Through imagination we fashion the novel reconstitution of elements of past experience so as to shape new potentials of and for experience. Such fashionings made by literature and the arts, it will be the contention of this book, present us with vital representations of the reality of experience by which we can construe our worlds; further, that the evidences of consciousness attended to by the arts and by literature are fuller representations than those offered in the partiality of abstract discourse and reasoning. For, made by all which is implied by psyche and not by mind alone, literature and the arts embody sense and sensuousness — sense embodied.

Divisions in the World of Experience

At the head of this chapter I referred to the objective world. Objective presumes subjective — and art products are often dismissed as mere expressions of the subjective personality. In an age of rationalism, and at the end of a decade in which the 'real world' has been handbagged, it is a serious falsification of the business of art and art-making. For it can easily consign, and in some quarters has easily consigned, art to the equivalent of decorative play, pleasant to look at or listen to or read, but essentially a spare-time activity of little consequence to the 'real world' of affairs, and certainly a diversion from the serious business of training young people to enter that world. Art in this perspective is viewed essentially either as relaxation or entertainment — with some, a social pursuit. It is what one does, or where one goes, in order to demonstrate a cultivated taste. (It is not without irony that the common metaphor here itself betokens consumption). Art is where one relaxes away from the world of Mammon — money, money-making, and the profit motive. Whilst accepting the importance of economics to everyone's life and the need to have some preparation for it, the potential world of experience is much vaster. It is surely a prime aim of education to provide child and adult alike with access to varieties of experience, not just the economic, in order to enrich in *all* ways the quality of living. Literature and the arts are potent means of enlarging experience, of engaging the actual experience of the student, and of making for awareness and understanding of self. But if the arts are to be given their important place in the development of young people, it is essential to counter the notion of their mere subjectivity and to show their educative potential in the development of the individual.

The encounter of which I write, the encounter with the reality of experience, provokes an attempt to relate, to connect. The encounter, for example, may be between the 'world-as-experienced' (until now) and the 'world-as-potential-for-experience'. Let us say, for example, that the present encounter is with the phenomenal world — a part of the world 'out there'. Let us say it is an encounter with a topography hitherto unknown. The subject (the person) encounters the object (the topography). If the encounter is to be creative there must be *engagement*; exactly such as an artist might bring to what he or she observes. The person is *active* in that meeting with the phenomenal world. But where the individual is passive, the encounter fails. We might even, in a small stretch of language, say that the topography (object) fails to *be* — for that person at least. There are some finely-drawn examples of just such failed encounters in Melvyn Bragg's splendid novel *The Maid of Buttermere* (1987). The following passage, much reduced, illustrates the theme:

> Hope stood on the point of Friar's Crag, looking down into the jaws of Borrowdale and had waited for the revelation; of scenes like these, great poets had written, great painters painted. Thomas Gray, on an ecstatic journey, had called this the vale of Elysium and after the publication of his popular journal letters, numerous writers had arrived to enquire into and celebrate the fascination and beauties of this divinely compacted complex of hills, valleys, streams, lakes and what Coleridge called 'their thrilling interspaces'...
>
> [Hope] had stood there looking at the prospect for a full three minutes. He had given it every chance, he thought: and the evening was a fine one... He would act out the phrases but all that had really impressed him was that fine stretch of water: he ought to be able to find some fine fishing.[4]

Hope had given *it*, the landscape, every chance. There has been no encounter, no active engagement. Hope has found only what he was looking for, some fine fishing. It requires a change in Hope, a recognition of the reality of his experience, before he can be active in the face of such an encounter, as indeed he is later in the novel. But at this stage in the career of his sensibility the potential for new experience remains unpossessed by Hope. The 'world', this particular portion of the world, to put the matter reductively, has achieved no subjective reality. The two polarities, of object and subject, remain apart, unconnected.

In creative encounter, therefore, I am going to suggest that the reciprocity of object (the world of experience or the world as experienced) and subject (the consciousness of the individual) demand a revised conception. One mediates the other: there is a dialectic between the polarities.

Traditionally, 'outer' phenomena are associated with 'objectivity' and 'inner' phenomena with 'subjectivity'. The terms presume separateness, even independence one from the other. They are concepts which have dominated our traditions of Western philosophic thought, and thereby the view we take of the reality of experience. Unchallenged, they carry some damaging implications for our conceptions of ourselves.

Echoing the words of the psycho-therapist Rollo May I shall begin with
the observation that what I am about to say

> ... may sound odd in the light of traditional academic psychology.
> It *should* sound strange. Our traditional psychology has been founded
> on the dichotomy between subject and object which has been the
> central characteristic of Western thought for the past four centuries.
> Ludwig Binswanger calls this dichotomy 'the cancer of all psycholo-
> gy and psychiatry up to now'. It is not avoided by behaviourism
> or operationalism, which would define experience only in objective
> terms. Nor is it avoided by isolating the creative experience as a
> purely subjective phenomenon.[5]

Out of the distinction between body and soul, mind and matter, Descartes fashioned his *Méthode* (1637). His *cogito ergo sum*, arrived at by a
process which has become known as Cartesian doubt, proceeds rom a
premise of the independence of mind and body. The existence of doubt
proves the existence of a doubter. Matter is more easily doubted than mind.
From these observations Descartes concluded:

> ... I was a substance whose essence or nature consists only in
> thinking, and which, that it may exist, has need of no place, nor is
> dependent on any material thing; so that 'I', that is to say, the mind
> by which I am that I am, is wholly distinct from the body, and is
> even more easily known than the latter, and is such, that although
> the fact were not, it would still continue to be all that is.[6]

Even the definition of 'I' ('the mind by which I am that I am'), it should
be noted, proceeds from a premissed dualism.[7]

Between the coarseness of material existence and the purity of the spirit
mediates human thought. Its sublime form is that Reason, which the late
seventeenth and early eighteenth centuries perfected into a cosmological
system of total explanation. In Cartesian philosophy the difference in things
became transmuted into the *independence* of things. So to conceive of the
nature of thought and cognition to be independent of all other things leads to
the indictment made by Jacques Maritain: '... the sin of Descartes is the sin
of *angelism*'.[8] It is the presumption of a free, spirit-like existence of the mind.

By so regarding mind and matter as discrete entities Descartes neglected
the properties of both as *processes*, related despite differences. Difference does
not necessarily denote complete separation. Even 'simple' concepts define
themselves against each other (woman/man, hot/cold) — and are, in
fact, polarities within larger concepts which subsume them both (human,
temperature).

The Dualism of Object and Subject

Traditional discriminations between 'object' and 'subject' derive from the
same principles of dualism. Once again, if we are to see the essential rela-

tionships which bind these categories, it may be larger, not smaller, concepts which are called for. Where it is presumed that the scientist scrutinizes the world of 'outer' phenomena, to make objective descriptions and explanations of reality, the psyche (that which seeks to know) is co-joined with that which is known. Seven decades back the distinguished physicist Arthur Eddington came to just such a conclusion. On the final page of his exposition of the physical world, in *Space, Time, and Gravitation* (1920), Eddington was impelled into this metaphysical speculation:

> All through the physical world runs that unknown content which must surely be the stuff of our consciousness. Here is a hint of aspects deep within the world of physics and yet unattainable by the method of physics. And, moreover, we have found that where science has progressed the farthest, the mind has but regained from nature that which the mind has put into nature. We have found a strange footprint on the shores of the unknown. We have devised profound theories, one after another, to account for its origin. At last, we have succeeded in reconstructing the creature that made the footprint. And lo! it is our own.[9]

Differently expressed, Eddington's insight has been refined by many notable thinkers who have observed that our constructions, even of the physical world, are endowed with conceptions of mind. The reality of 'outer' phenomena, their presumed objective being, achieve their nature by virtue of the 'inner' reality of the conceptualizer, his or her subjectivity. The same event may be miracle to one and rationally-explicable phenomenon to another. Hope fails to see, in the landscape of Borrowdale (Bragg, 1987), the realities to which others attested, because he can not *conceive* those realities. It is the encounter of consciousness with Chaos which makes Cosmos, which makes pattern, design, construction, so that the world of experience may acquire meaning.

What is significant in the Eddington excerpt is the clear association of 'inner' and 'outer' realities. The knower and the known, as Marjorie Grene powerfully argued in her influential work,[10] exist in a symbiotic relationship. If 'inner' and 'outer' realities may have some kind of mutual dependence, so may the reality of experience be known in combinations of the objective and the subjective. That objectivity and subjectivity may well influence, or interfere with each other, is well recognized in many circumstances. Commonly, for some operations of thinking, we are counselled to 'keep our feelings out of it' or are told 'not to get emotional'. Rationality is presumed to be cognition freed from any affect. But there is a contrary truth too. *Right* thinking, as compared with purely rational thinking, may need to take account of feeling and emotion as well. To produce an entirely logical conclusion may be *inappropriate*, simply because the human condition exceeds that of the exclusively rational; the appropriate conclusion must 'feel' right, not simply be logically demonstrable. The satires of Dean Swift show just this. Through the suppression of feeling-responses, as in *A Modest Proposal* (1729), an entirely logical argument develops. The presentation is reasoned.

But logic and reasoning are simply operations. They denote *how* one performs a kind of thinking upon selected contents.

The products of reason can be only as good as that matter which they take into the reckoning, and upon which the logics and operations of reasoning are then performed. Yet the almost axiomatic faith in the supremacy of reason can lead astray. It is why, for example, intuition is so distrusted; by its very nature intuition does not conform to the pattern of logical thinking or deductive reasoning. Intuition omits or bypasses those stages of logical sequencing by which arguments of reason proceed. This is so, whether or not the intuition proves to be just, whether or not the omitted stages of the argument can or can not be determined. One's intuition may lead astray; that is true. Equally true is the fact that one's reasoning can lead astray. But perceived only as opportunities for the exercise of reason and logic, some conditions and problems are not seen at all. There is a variety of means by which we come to terms with experience. To seek to edit all human means of coming into possession of experience by the criteria of reason alone — itself an operation which will not infallibly produce pertinent and acceptable answers — is to seek to dehumanize.

There is a contrary truth, (as all such truths, conditional upon circumstance) that refers to contexts in which features of the psyche, other than those of the reasoning capacity alone, must be involved, if the individual is to operate effectively. Rollo May (1976) once more:

> There are now data in Rorschach tests, for example, that indicate that people can more accurately observe precisely when they are emotionally involved — that is, reason works better when emotions are present; the person sees sharper and more accurately when his emotions are engaged. Indeed, we cannot really see an object unless we have some emotional involvement with it. [11]

Creative Encounter

'Inner' and 'outer', 'subjective' and 'objective' are, in fact, blurred definitions which the scientist can no longer ignore. [12] 'Subjective' and 'objective' are categories of experience which so-called depth psychologists have had to break down for the purposes of both analysis and therapy. [13] Such conceptual divisions break down in that encounter which creatively attends to the world of experience. They dissolve in the act of attending to whatever range of experience, personality, and the occasion of the moment afford.

A creative encounter engages psyche with the reality of experience. In this encounter the conscious person, the 'subjective' polarity in the encounter, is *attending* to the world of experience (the summation of personality), the 'objective' polarity. It is an act of self-consciousness. Of course, the entirety of experience will not be available in any one moment, but connections among and between elements of experience will almost inevitably occur in the encounter.

In this encounter object and subject engage reciprocally. One may know the world of experience objectively, in the shape of thoughts and ideas, or subjectively in the form of images and feelings. Already the functioning of consciousness can no longer be supported by a simple, bipartite division of the subject's mental construct of the object's 'out-thereness'. The object (that which is known or which comes into awareness) is not independent of the subject (that which knows or seeks to know), for the very reason which Coleridge expressed: 'To know is in its very essence a verb active'.[14] To know is an activity of consciousness, a movement towards comprehension.

In Coleridge's speculations it is the vitality of the interaction between the objectivity and subjectivity of knowing which provides important clues as to the nature of the creative encounter.[15]

From his insights into the essential relationship of object and subject — the means by which each is a realization of the other — proceed those constructions, 'between thought and reality', which bind the knower and the known. Coleridge termed that space between the thought and the reality an 'intermundium'. The projection, or product, which occupies that space may be variously named. John Fowles, for example, in 'Notes on an Unfinished Novel' (1969), preferred the term 'metaphor':

> One cannot describe reality; only give metaphors that indicate it. All human modes of description (photographic, mathematical and the rest, as well as literary) are metaphorical. Even the most precise scientific description of an object or movement is a tissue of metaphors.[16]

In Fowles's vocabulary it is the 'metaphor' which stands between the thought and the reality, the metaphor which is the means by which the thought *of* the reality is embodied. His reference to scientific description reminds us of the fact that in purely scientific contexts it is now well understood that there is an intimate connection of conception and elaboration of thinking between metaphor, theory, and model.[17] In some instances, indeed, it is difficult to separate the metaphor from the theory being advanced, since the model on which the theory depends for its hypothesizing, deduction, and falsifiability is itself perceived, and articulated, in the device of metaphor. For metaphor is not simply an illustration of the given case, but the *organizing principle* of the data which constitutes the cognition. Metaphor has *function*, not merely decorative style. Metaphors not only represent (i.e. re-present to consciousness) thought as symbolic articulation; they are the means by which the proposing and advancing of that thought becomes possible. It is a recognition which has crucial significance for works of art, as well; each work of art is the metaphor containing the perceptions and cognitions on which it is founded and from which it is made.

Art and the Integration of Experience

The space of the intermundium taken up by the work of art references the world of personal experience. That fabrication (poem, play, dance, painting, sculpture, film ...), the intermundium of Coleridge, the metaphor of Fowles, has *intelligibility*. The work of art, to switch now to the term employed by Roland Barthes, is a 'simulacrum', made not in order to reproduce a copy of life, of events, of experience, but *in order to make sense*. For the product of the artistic encounter with the reality of experience is, again in Barthes's words (from his essay 'The Structuralist Activity' (1963)), 'intellect added to object'.

Artworks bring into an essential relationship object and subject: they are not only the products of that interaction, but are vital means of bringing the relationship into being. They mediate consciousness and the world of experience. In ways which differ according to the type of art and the forms of their evolving, they provide for a transcription of the reality of that world of experience. They embody not merely subjective responses to that world, but are objectifications of it, and are movements towards awareness, knowledge, and comprehension.

W.H. Auden made exactly the same point in his essay of 1935, 'Psychology and Art Today'.[18] Art, for Auden, was 'more than an autobiographical record'. It employs the personal, the autobiographical. But because, as Auden also says, the artist is *active with experience*, not merely a passive amenuensis of that experience, the artwork should be viewed as 'deliberate phantasy directed towards understanding'. It is important to recall that Auden does not intend phantasy to be taken as escapist illusion or delusion, but as the product of imaginative creation (from its Greek and Latin roots 'a making visible'). It may be recalled, too, that Auden in this same essay posits the notion of 'parable-art' as a consequence of the shaping of phantasy towards understanding. That is, that the artwork which results stands in some way not as a unique testament to the individual experience, but somehow transcends it, so that it gathers representativeness; a notion close to the intention of Fowles's 'metaphor'. Highly particular, even autobiographical, the shaping of experience into art achieves a larger reference with which others can identify. Joyce's Bloom, minutely detailed, highly individual, becomes Everyman. That is true whether or not one has a predilection for kidneys fried in butter...

The artistic encounter with the reality of experience brings into play thoughts, ideas, feelings, imaginings, and sensings of consciousness. The great advantage of these products of art and literature resides in the fact that they range freely across the gamut of consciousness: they employ, but are not confined to, evidences of the intellect alone. Intelligence is a larger concept than that of intellect — one which allows, for example, the direct sensuous apprehension of experience. Art-making is an activity which not only influences what the mind apprehends and knows, but creatively brings into consciousness, and therefore into the mind's prospective consideration, the very means by which consciousness is itself constituted:

> For to us the self-consciousness is not a kind of *being*, but a kind of *knowing*, and that too the highest and furthest that exists for us.[19]

In art-making the workaday distinctions between 'inner' and 'outer' realities dissolve in the creative encounter. I.A. Richards's explication of Coleridge's speculations is both precise and a summary of the integration of experience achieved in the finished work:

[Coleridge's] subject-object machinery introduces no such split between the ingredients of the mind. It is for him an instrument of
noting and insisting, that nothing of which we are in any way
conscious is *given* to the mind. Into the simplest seeming 'datum' a
constructing, forming activity from the mind has entered. And the
perceiving and the forming are the same. The subject (the self) has
gone into what it perceives, and what it perceives is, in this sense,
itself. So the object becomes the subject and the subject the object.
And as, to understand what Coleridge is saying, we must not take
the object as something given to us; so equally we must not take the
subject to be a mere formless void out of which all things myster-
iously and ceaselessly rush to become everything we know. The
subject is what it is through the objects it has been.[20]

It is through this very integration, the dissolution of object and subject,
that we are enabled to sense the unity of a work of art, its *gestalt*. Objective
and subjective experience are united, or reunited. There is wholeness. It is the
wholeness of experience which enables us, without divorce or contradiction,
to hold 'objective' experience and 'subjective' response simultaneously. A
knowledge of photosynthesis should not detract from our perception of the
beauty of trees; nor atomic concepts from the awe sensed in the viewing of a
rainbow:

> Even the rainbow has a body
> made of the drizzling rain
> and is an architecture of glistening atoms
> built up, built up
> yet you can't lay your hand on it,
> nay, nor even your mind.

> D.H. Lawrence, 'The Rainbow'[21]

In creative encounter consciousness shapes and adapts the reality of
experience, a reality which is an interaction of thought and thing:

> ... object and subject, being and knowing, are identical, each in-
> volving and supposing the other. In other words, it is a subject
> which becomes a subject by the act of constructing itself objectively
> to itself; but which is never an object except for itself, and only so far
> as by the very same act it becomes a subject.[22]

Art objects, as we may now very precisely speak of them, are creations
made as a way of knowing. This is, in itself, an important justification for
the arts, at all levels of education, and one endorsed in the influential
Gulbenkian Report: *The Arts in Schools* (1982). In the present climate of
educational change, and the instrumental thinking which would fashion it,
the significance of the experience of art (its making and its remaking through
expressive activity) needs to be presented decisively, without apology, and
without its subversion to other ulterior and utilitarian purposes ('doing art'

will help you in industrial design, making poems will help you write a letter of application...). For the intelligence, as Coleridge usually referred to the capacity for self-knowing, both discovers and displays itself through realizations of the Imagination. In those projections which are art, the imagination blends subject and object, reconciling the knower and the known through the *essemplastic* power of that faculty to blend into one. Through the imagination one projects mind upon the world, creating that interaction by which one will come to know the reality of experience; one's own, and that of others.

At the end of *A Portrait of the Artist As A Young Man* (1916), Stephen Daedalus declares: 'Welcome, O life! I go to encounter for the millionth time the reality of experience...'[23] The encounter includes that which is known and, through the encounter, that which is presently unknown. The known includes data and perceptions of the world, together with those thoughts and systems of belief which inform experience and seek to explain our world. There is the unknown (the adventure of life itself, as Stephen recognizes), potentials of experience which one's living may encounter, together with the not-yet-known, previous experience unconsciously or subliminally held. As these active participles of experience emerge into awareness, so may the conscious personality play over them and determine their significance as they combine and relate to other known possessions of the reality of experience. Without the constructing agency of imagination the world of experience would remain indissolubly a shifting, meaningless flux of impression. Through the imagination disparate elements of experience are related and coherence induced where reason alone seeks to categorize and segregate. And through the art of the imagination, the conscious mind then *recognizes*, in the full implication of the word, the reality of experience.

Notes and References

1 Barthes, R. (1985) *Grain of the Voice*, trans. Coverdale, L., London, Jonathan Cape, p. 8.
2 I am aware that there is a state of dreaming in which one becomes aware of oneself in the act of dreaming, and can then 'enter' the dream, participating in it and even shaping the dream as one would wish it to go. I think this partly-conscious mode of dreaming, preceding wakefulness, does not detract from the general point that dreaming is involuntary, not an act of will. In this special case the purposiveness of willed intervention follows, during part-consciousness, the involuntary duration of the dream.
3 The final *reductio* of *all* knowledge would perhaps reveal something taken-for-granted, as Louis Arnaud Reid proposed: '*All* knowledge contains an intuitive element or factor.' 'The Arts Within a Plural Concept of Knowledge', in Abbs, P. (Ed.) (1989) *The Symbolic Order*, London, Falmer Press, p. 15.
4 Bragg, M. (1987) *The Maid of Buttermere*, London, Hodder and Stoughton, pp. 50–1.
5 May, R. (1976) *The Courage to Create*, London, Collins, p. 49.
6 Descartes, R. (1912) *Discourse on Method*, trans. Veitch, J., London, Everyman, Dent, p. 27.
7 Logical reasoning might further note, as Bertrand Russell pointed out, that

Descartes 'nowhere proves that thoughts need a thinker, nor is there reason to believe this except in a grammatical sense' (Russell, B. (1961) *History of Western Philosophy*, 2nd. edn., London, Allen and Unwin, p. 550). In turn we might say that the proofs of reason *alone* again seem very partial.

8   Maritain, J. (1928) 'Descartes', in *Three Reformers*, London, Sheed and Ward, p. 54. The argument is further elaborated pp. 54–81.

9   Eddington, A. (1920) *Space, Time and Gravitation*, Cambridge, Cambridge University Press.

10 Grene, M. (1966) *The Knower and the Known*, London, Faber and Faber.

11 May, R., *op. cit.*, p. 49.

12 See, for example, Polanyi, M. (1958) *Personal Knowledge*, London, Routledge and Kegan Paul.

13 See, for example, Hillman, J. (1962) *Emotion*, 2nd. edn., London, Routledge and Kegan Paul, esp. pp. 95–6.

14 Watson, G. (Ed.) (1965) *Biographia Literaria*, corrected edn., London, Dent, p. 150.

15 I have previously traced the outline of Coleridge's reflections on the inter-relationship of subject and object in Webb, E. '*Reality's Dark Dream*: Coleridge's Language of Consciousness', *Critical Quarterly*, **25**, no. 1.

16 Fowles, J. (1969) 'Notes on an Unfinished Novel', in Bradbury, M. (Ed.) (1977) *The Novel Today*, London, Fontana, p. 139.

17 An extended elaboration of this notion in the context of science was made by Hesse, M.B. (1966) *Models and Metaphors in Science*, Indiana, Notre Dame, see esp. pp. 164–5. Of the same decade, and the first to propose an 'interactional' view of metaphor, was Black, M. (1962), 'Metaphor', *Models and Metaphors*, Ithaca and London, Cornell University Press.

18 Auden, W.H. 'Psychology and Art Today', in Mendelson, E. (Ed.) (1977) *The English Auden*, London, Faber and Faber, pp. 332–42.

19 Coleridge, S.T. *Biographia Literaria*, *op. cit.*, xii, p. 152.

20 Richards, I.A. (1950) *Coleridge on Imagination*, 2nd. edn., London, Routledge and Kegan Paul, pp. 56–7.

21 From de Sola Pinto, V. and Roberts, W. (Eds) (1972) *The Complete Poems of D.H. Lawrence*, revised edn., 2 vols., London, Heinemann, vol. II, p. 692.

22 Coleridge, S.T. *op. cit.*, p. 152.

23 Joyce, J. (1960), *A Portrait of the Artist As A Young Man*, Harmondsworth, Penguin, p. 253.

Chapter 2

À la Recherche du Temps: Memory and the Making of the Historical Present

> Imagination is our means of interpreting the world, and it is *also* our means of forming images in the mind. The images themselves are not separate from our interpretations of the world; they are our way of thinking of the objects in the world. We see the forms in the mind's eye and we see these very forms in the world. We could not do one of these things if we could not do the other. The two abilities are joined in our ability to understand that the forms have a certain meaning, that they are always significant of something beyond themselves.
>
> Mary Warnock[1]

Realizations of Experience

All creative encounter makes for something new. Whatever else is made new there is always new awareness. 'I hadn't realized that before' is itself a statement which confers reality, which brings forth into being by bringing forth into awareness. It is a personal cognition. Such realizations can take many forms, from the casual to the highly-elaborated. In creative encounter such realizations may result in the making of art objects. What they realize is the active and shaping quest of psyche to explore and embody the reality of experience.

There is, first, encounter with one's own reality of the moment; the perceptions, sensory impressions, feelings and thoughts of the immediate present — the awareness of one's condition *now*. There is memory, with which any artistic encounter will necessarily engage; the memory of events, thoughts, dreams, knowledge — of oneself and others, the knowledge of facts and other histories ... all of that which makes up the individual's world of experience and which may be consciously retrieved or involuntarily presented to regions of consciousness. By memory I here mean an inclusive reference: to all of that which is called to mind, prompted by or through association with the present immediate experience.

The great discovery of Freud was the discovery of memory; not the fact that humans could recall past events, but the extensive and *active* nature of memory. For memory, as Freud discovered, does not 'sleep', as it were, lying inert and comatose awaiting its awakening by some act of will. In ways not always understood by the individual, personal memory powerfully shapes our sense of being here and now — even, and sometimes especially — when memory is submerged. In the artistic encounter there is engagement with memory to reveal and to make available possessions of personal biography which will assist in the exploration of the present experience.

Sometimes the past and the present are coterminous, both immediately present, as it were, without any discernible time-lag. The experience 'now' recalls instantly the past. On other occasions the associations and connections of memory are not known until the particular experience has itself become a part of memory. Not until after the event, do we realize what we have been through. The circumstance of the time *at that time* was unacknowledged, its significance within experience not noted. So there may be a delay, a lapse of time between any immediate experience, and the later recall of that experience. It may then emerge into mind already cast alongside other contributions of memory.

In artistic encounter there is both active recall and unconscious association of other experience which stands alongside, and is somehow implicated within, the cause of the immediately present experience which the art works over. But it is not simple recall. It is recollection; a gathering together of past impressions, previous thoughts, suggestive images ... all of which, often intuitively, are sensed to attach to the initiating experience. There is acceptance and rejection by the artist at some stage in the composing of the work-in-progress. Some offerings of memory, at first rejected, may well find their way into the final work. Others at first selected will have to be excised. There is clearly at work an editing procedure, which will proceed according to both the relevance of what is recalled and its usefulness to the artist in the expression of the projected work. Such recollects of past experience do more than that, I am going to suggest. For such recollects of previous experience *actively explore the nature of the new experience in order that it may achieve definition.*

Memory and Artistic Encounter

The place of memory in artistic encounter operates in several ways. It may indeed use previously-formed thoughts, intellectual predispositions towards one or another kind of realization. But it employs above all else, I believe, that special memory which we call Imagination. What I shall here outline has pertinence to all of the art-forms; but I write particularly of literature, and within that context, the poem and poetry-making. The inquiry will therefore also suggest certain points of departure for the appreciation of poetry, and thus to its teaching.

In his *Biographia Literaria* (1817) (ch. xiv) Coleridge wrote of the sub-ordination 'according to their relative worth and dignity' of all of the faculties of the poet. In part he is calling to mind that 'integration of personality' which characterizes and goes alongside the act of making itself. Copious testimonial evidences of this state have been gathered previously by Rosa-mund Harding,[2] so we may here by-pass them, taking them collectively as a broad depiction of the condition of the psyche during the making procedure of art. This aspect of the integration of the maker of art begins to assemble an answer to Coleridge's question 'What is a Poet?' His own suggestions, more tentative, as to 'What is a Poem?' concentrate upon the 'interpenetration' of the constituent parts of experience, an assembly via which the completed poem projects its own identity. Assembled *out of* experience, it *becomes* experience. It achieves a wholeness which we could perhaps more easily denote as a Gestalt. It is an ordering of experience.

In its ordering and sequencing, however, a poem clearly exceeds, and in many ways is different from, the fragmentary and spontaneous experience-of-the-moment — the actuality of real-time events. A poem is therefore an active gathering together (recollection) of experience, rather than the simple and direct representation of experience. As such it is a special kind of history: it embodies not only those sense-impressions of the moment, such as com-pose incident and event, it gathers to itself also a larger frame of reference derived from the total experience, the psychobiography, of the poet.

Whilst undergoing its various states of work-in-progress, a poem is already a predator of past experience, accumulating to itself certain of those products of that active experimentation which is a significant feature of all composing. Since the identity of a poem (or any art object) can not be known fully in advance of its 'discovery' by the very processes which will shape it, even as they explore its features, and explore as they shape, the emerging poem opportunely raids past experience. This is true even where the artist works to a fully-programmed brief in the *transcription* of the piece. Here we may think of Mozart 'spontaneously' drafting his scores. In fact, the activity of composing *preceded* the scoring. The active combination of musical images, the delimitation of the structure of the piece, even the particularities of the arrangement, were known in advance. They had already been worked out in the composer's head; the selection, rejection, modifying, and experi-mentation which other composers would have had to conduct on paper, (the classic case is no less a person than Beethoven) in Mozart's case were mentally arrived at. The genius of Mozart, in this context, is his prodigious musical memory. He could store away in his memory the version of a work decided upon, the entire musical invention and improvisation of that work having already been gone through mentally. Hence he was able to conduct conversa-tions with people, including his wife, whilst he wrote out the score — the physical transcription of memory. In a somewhat similar way we know that Charles Dickens shared in this facility for writing out in company, and joining in the conversation, sections of novels already composed. One may think also of Milton, gone blind, dictating the composition of *Paradise Lost*. In more recent decades William Golding has written of tracing over the words which were already there, on the paper, so detailed was his own 'pro-gramme' by which the novel had been designed. It is important, therefore, to distinguish between individual procedures which vary from one artist to another, and those processes of composing which feature in all art-making and which may go on at all times, whether or not the artist is actually at work on the piece and committing the composition to paper.

During *this* stage of making the composition, almost all artists would testify to a sense of surprise, a discovery of something which they did not know was 'there' — the existence of which may be helpful or a distraction. James Joyce made a habit of collecting these discoveries. He called them his 'epiphanies'; and his collecting of them suggests that with him artistic composing went on more or less uninterruptedly — a conscious collecting of experience, as it were. More commonly, however, the surprises issue out of the very act of attempting to make the artwork. I must let the following testimony stand as representative of the nature of this experience. During the improvisation of a poem (usually called the 'drafting') the processes of making the piece discover these surprises, as retold in this account by the distinguished Australian poet A.D. Hope:

> As for the poet, he has to learn to be conscious of the effect as a whole but he is rarely aware of the details of his 'score'. He works by habit and trial and error, until he recognises the effect he is searching for ... It is a sense that a poet can only learn by patience, persistence and alertness. There are no rules for it and no prescriptions; because one has to be able to recognise the 'rightness' of something not existing before its moment of emergence, and often in a context not yet clear to the composer. The composition of a poem is a series of epiphanies.[3]

The artist, at various stages in the composing, 'recognises the effect he is searching for...'. What is being searched for is something which in a paradoxical way is already 'there'. But where? In the reality of experience, in a projection of experience which is inferentially held, as some kind of memory against which the vocalization of the speech of the poem is tested. If we follow through the discursive line drawn by A.D. Hope, the clear suggestion is that the poet is attempting to organize something which has, in an as yet unrealized region of consciousness, already happened. We can recall the assertion of Michelangelo that the sculpture on which he worked was already 'there' in the block of Carrera marble, and that his task was to reveal its presence. We might recall, too, that the origin of 'poem' is in the Greek *poiema*, 'something made', and 'poet' in the Greek *poietes* refers to 'the maker' or artificer. What is being made is a representation of the reality of experience — a reality already felt or intuited, but important enough to demand of its maker a fabrication which will do justice to the memory of experience. The act or process of bringing something before one's mind in such a way that one apprehends it, and the act of making oneself conscious of something, are both variant definitions of what 'realization' is. Just as all memories may be far more than direct, literal imprints of the past, so too the 'memory' which is to be projected in the form of a poem (or any other art form) must first be organized.

History in the Present Tense

'Memory' is always an encounter with the present. At its simplest it is a recall required for immediate purposes, let us say a fact which is required. Where the recall is of personal history, however, what memory supplies is most likely to be far more than the simple facts of the matter. On some occasions establishing the facts of the matter, even for oneself, may demand a disentangling or a reworking of experience. Thus one, to some degree, rewrites personal history. How else would we be able to take a different view of events in our past? Memory, mediated by history, is glossed by the present. Memory searches out its impressions; as these gather, a network of relationships is formed which then more clearly defines the emerging context. This seems to be what, in A.D. Hope's account, is being tested out by the poet, against that which, in its inception, persisted as a vague impression only. Yet, however vague this first impression, its very persistence acts as a focus for the composing. Cézanne fixes upon a tree, Yeats upon the working metaphor of the falcon and the falconer, John Fowles upon the image of a woman in black standing at the end of the Cobb. There is something 'there' which enables, perhaps even impels, the selective association of memory to operate and the making of the composition to proceed.

There is recollection, and there is re-collection — that dynamic accumulation, selection and rejection, from which the poem will evolve. Stephen Spender, in his article 'The Making of a Poem', affirms this sense of the poem somehow already being 'there' within the matrix of memory, and he is clear on the nature of that poetic memory:

> If the art of concentrating in a particular way is the discipline necessary for poetry to reveal itself, memory exercised in a particular way is the natural gift of poetic genius. The poet, above all else, is a person who never forgets certain sense-impressions which he has experienced and which he can re-live again and again as though with all their original freshness.[4]

The memory of which Spender writes is a memory *for* experience, rather than a memory *of* experience — referring not simply to what memory contains, but to the way that memory works; a memory predisposed towards the collection and storing of sense-impression as mental image. It is memory founded in the sensuous character of experience itself, rather than one operating by recall of abstracting generalizations. In art it is the combining of these sensuous impressions, in new contexts as well as in those of their origination, which is the particular function of the Imagination.

To see this memory in operation it is necessary to see 'image' in a light rather different from that usually cast by notions of the '*poetic* image', where what is usually being referred to is the power of a particular image within the text to 'suggest', to subsume and summarize, regions of meaning which tremble on the verge of conceptualization. Such poetic images signify but do not say; in this resides a great deal of their potency and their immediacy. They connect directly with the sensuous experience of the reader. Therefore, what I have to say in no way diminishes from the importance of the image cast as poetic. What I wish to direct attention to, at this stage, is image in a simpler sense, not the semantics of the image, but its origin.

Images, at a simple level, may be taken as representations of residual sense-impressions. They may be memories which correspond to a single sense mode; in more complex organizations they combine two or more sense modes within a single impression. At a high level of organization they may become the organizing principle of an art product.

Imagination, seen in this way, is concerned with the *processing* of experience, the means by which memory records experience. It is the raid upon memory, consciously or unconsciously, which produces these images which then call the artist's conscious attention to themselves as potential contributors and realizers of the work-in-progress. It is imagination, seen now as the active working-over of these images of memory, which will direct them — selecting, modifying, arranging, and (recalling Coleridge's expression) synthesizing them. As they are so directed, so do these images of experience set the scene, as it were, for the emerging work, and begin to stage the show. As they are deployed, so do they begin to realize the context of the experience not yet realized.

Sensory Experience and its Images

In one of the vocabularies of psychology, mental images belong to two broad categories. 'Percepts' relate to the experience of the moment, 'seeing' in the present tense what is there.[5] Such images, as are present to the eye of the beholder, apply similarly to those images which are percepts of the other sense modes: images of the direct sensory experience of hearing, touch, taste, smell, and movement. 'Recollects', however, are experiences of the image (of different sensory types) not actually present in the immediate environment. These 'not here not now' images derive from previous perceptual experience, but are reproduced in the absence of the original sensory stimulation. These are the memory images.

It is important to bear in mind, of course, that memory images may not be absolutely faithful reproductions of the original perceptual experience. Memory images *may* replicate with exactness. But as soon as perceptual images begin to lodge in memory, they are subject to possible change. They are subject to the same factors of change to which all memory is liable — not only its fallibility and capacity for decay, but also its amendment with the changing circumstances of one's living. Memory images may represent themselves as amalgams of a variety of separate experiences. When recalled they betoken not simply a given, isolated experience, but a range of experience derived from a variety of circumstances. Such images frequently have acquired, through memory as the agency of personality, another order of pertinence — one we might refer to as the private or personal semantics of the image. They are loaded now with significance, or 'meaning', or a potential for meaning. *Memory images accumulate experience*: the detritus of past experience may be pulled to them by a kind of gravitational influence. And this is so even if one 'can't quite say' what that pertinence is. There is a suggestive force to them, as T.S. Eliot noted of an author's imagery which comes from the whole of his sensitive life since early childhood. Why, for all of us, out of all that we have heard, seen, felt, in a lifetime, do certain images recur, charged with emotion, rather than others? The song of one bird, the leap of one fish, at a particular place and time, the scent of one flower, an old woman on a German mountain path, six ruffians seen through an open window playing cards at night at a small French railway junction where there was a water-mill: such memories may have symbolic value, but of what we cannot tell, for they come to represent the depths of feeling into which we cannot peer.[6]

There is often a very close connection between Eliot's critical reflections and the practice of his own poetry making, the criticism issuing out of matters posed in the composition of the poems. This reflection on mental imagery clearly references Eliot's poem 'Journey of the Magi' (1927), a poem written six years before the appearance of the essay from which the passage above has been extracted. The passage not only illuminates something of the history which went into the making of a particular poem; it has general interest too. For images which recur, 'charged with emotion' as Eliot expressed it, do so because somehow they have *value* to the individual; they are important. That is so even if — especially if — 'we cannot tell' what they represent. We cannot tell, I am going to suggest, because the image *on its own* lacks context; only its location (or relocation) within a matrix of reference, which accommodates it, will transform feeling to meaning. Some images, when located in such a scheme of reference, will then be charged with exclusively personal meaning. Others may emerge into meanings which are symbolic, not necessarily or exclusively esoteric. The context for the location of images such as these, even though they have their origin in events personally witnessed, is outside of the narrowly biographical. There are things which one has seen and heard which, in themselves and for us personally, we might say, signify nothing. Put that experience into another context, however, and such images can emerge transformed with a charged significance. Eliot's own poem, 'The Journey of the Magi' — the first poem he had attempted for two years — itself demonstrates the symbolic transformation of meaning when personal experience (several of the images he cites in the reflection) is located in another context.

There are, clearly, differences in personal imaging; both in the sense-type and the degree or strength of its operation. It may well be that artists 'select' (or have chosen for them) the particular art forms on which they will concentrate because of that sense-mode, or combination of sense-modes, which in them is most highly developed. What is certainly true, however, is that there are differences in the acuity of our perceptions of the moment, and in the extent to which we are able to summon to mind those recollects of past experience. Some senses, and therefore their after-the-event memory images, remain relatively undeveloped. Some might well atrophy with age.

With age, for example, it might be the perception of smell which is blunted (in fact this is the case for most people as they become elderly). Alongside the diminishing perception of the moment might well go a de-creased ability to recall past sensory impressions of the type. If the memory image (the recollect) fades, then not only is the sensory image lost, but the memories attaching to it have dissolved also. On the other hand 'the scent of one flower', to take one of the examples offered by Eliot, may retain its perfume, its percept still be sharp for us, but the context which memory once supplied has faded:

> As for myself,
> Where first I met the bitter scent is lost.
> I, too, often shrivel the grey shreds,
> Sniff them and think and sniff again and try
> Once more to think what it is I am remembering,
> Always in vain. I cannot like the scent,
> Yet I would rather give up others more sweet,
> With no meaning, than this bitter one.
>
> I have mislaid the key. I sniff the spray
> And think of nothing; I see and I hear nothing;
> Yet seem, too, to be listening, lying in wait
> For what I should, yet never can, remember ...

> Edward Thomas: from 'Old Man'[7]

Image and memory may be tightly bonded, or they can drift apart. Edward Thomas's fine poem exemplifies a common experience — the 'can't quite say' of a past experience which has somehow been triggered by an event or perception in the present moment. Yet there is 'meaning' some-where in the past — to take the clear inference from Thomas's poem that he would rather give up other scents 'with no meaning'. In this case the percept (the 'bitter scent' of the moment) is sharp enough: it is the memory prompt-ed, once prompted, by this sense-impression which has faded. So the poem recollects the inability to remember.

The confrontation between the past, however recent, and the present is a continuously active encounter. It is where we make sense of experience, or attempt to — sometimes failing, as Edward Thomas's poem demonstrates. Where the present reconstitutes its encounters with the past it generates histories — versions of the past seen in the perspective of the present. It is not without significance here to note that the almost automatic tense of the lyric poem, unlike the narrative poem, is the present tense. Narratives, in prose and in verse, adopt the past tense — because here the sense of completion is vital. Lyric poems celebrate the moment, narratives celebrate a succession of moments, of events. The lyric impulse pulls a moment out of time, so to scrutinize it. A narrative must be ended before it can begin to make sense. There are, of course, exceptions to this general formulation — exceptions which are often deliberately experimental in their attempts to break down, or break away from, these time-realizations. Yet such attempts themselves work, when they do work, because the mode of exposition is played off against their habitual tenses.

Memory images, as the sense-impressions of past experience, might sharpen or blunt the percepts of the moment. Memory can always get in the way of present experience. The perception of the moment may be pre-conditioned by the past or recollects of the past. We see most clearly what we are looking for; we hear most audibly what we are listening for. In both cases what we are actually doing is scanning the present, not for its own unique characteristics, but for its resemblances and correspondences to a memory-bank of previous images and memories. What is true of the two sense modes of sight and sound, the two which are generally the most highly developed in most people, is true, too, of those other sense-impressions we collect as tactile, olfactory, gustatory, and kinaesthetic images.

The Nature of Mental Imagery

It may be useful briefly to reflect generally upon the nature of mental imagery. We all use mental images of sense-impressions, and some people have highly developed and trained recollections of sense experience. The musician, for example, whether as performer or composer, quite clearly has a developed and trained perception of sound, a precise recollection of sound images. Performance and rehearsal are sustained attempts to match the present production against an idealised version of sound images. These are aural images projected out of a mental repertoire of experience. A good car mechanic has a developed memory pattern for sound against which to tune the present perception of engine noises. Further, the sounds emitted by the engine provide important diagnostic evidences. To take another example: I recall talking with a chef in his kitchen. Having popped one dish into the oven, he was busily engaged on a variety of other tasks, getting other dishes prepared. When he took the first dish out of the oven, I asked him how he knew it was 'done'. 'Because it smells right' was his answer. In a similar fashion I watched him 'measure' ingredients by a combination of the visual and the tactile ('about this much') rather than by actual measurement of weight and volume. Wine-, tea-, and coffee-tasters in a similar way must have highly developed memory images of the gustatory and olfactory senses, together with visual perceptions.

From these examples, among many others which might be cited, it is possible to appreciate how prevalent, indeed essential, is the employment of mental imagery in a wide variety of trades, professions, and arts. On many occasions the mental images are employed quite unconsciously, of course. They are sublimated in the skill of actually doing something; indeed, one sign of skill in most contexts is just this seeming ease or effortlessness of the performance. In such cases the processing of mental images is not as obvious as in the case of the apprentice, novice, or beginner who is still in the process of acquiring the skill. But in the arts, in all the arts, percept and recollect of the various sense modes operate in vital ways. It is in the use and deployment of such images that much of the sensuousness of art resides, distinguishing it from the didactic and expository modes of making meaning. For in art the images of the art-form enable us to make an immediate sensuous apprehension. This is not to say that we will immediately *understand* a given work, that we shall be able to render it into paraphraseable meaning. But it does mean, as Eliot said of the poem, that we shall be able to appreciate it before we come to comprehend it.

For the poet too, while rehearsing a poem during its many stages of composition, is almost certainly operating with some degree of unconscious internalization. There will also be, in most cases, periods of sustained attention when recollects of sense-impression taken into the emerging work will be subjected to deliberate scrutiny, analysis, and editing.

It is here, in the searching for alternatives, that an induction of previous perceptual experience will be entailed. For some poets it might be that recollects of certain sense-impressions dominate others. Some poets have an ease of access into particular sense modes. It could be revealing criticism to determine what these are, characteristically, in the work as a whole of a given poet. In the case of any given poem, however, we should certainly give directed attention to the nature and range of its sense-images.

Take, for example, Yeats's sonnet 'Leda and the Swan' (1923). It might be a commonplace of criticism — though I have not seen it expressed in quite this way — that the poem depends heavily upon kinaesthetic images for its realization. To illustrate the point I have italicised in the following reprint what seem to me to be some of the most pertinent images. In the classroom it would, of course, be my students who would make these selections as a means of promoting awareness and generating consequent discussion:

> A sudden *blow*: the great wings *beating* still
> Above the *staggering* girl, her thighs *caressed*
> By the dark webs, her nape *caught* in his bill,
> He *holds* her helpless breast upon his breast.
>
> How can those terrified vague fingers *push*
> The feathered glory from her *loosening* thighs?
> And how can body, *laid* in that white rush,
> But *feel* the strange heart *beating* where it lies?
>
> A *shudder* in the loins engenders there
> The broken wall, the burning roof and tower
> And Agamemnon dead.
> Being so *caught* up,
> So *mastered* by the brute blood of the air,
> Did she *put on* his knowledge with his power
> Before the indifferent beak could *let her drop*?
>
> W.B. Yeats[8]

We classify at our peril, it is true; and our classifications are notional, not absolute. They are provisional, merely means *towards* a recognition, not the particularity of the experience itself. Nonetheless, in general terms it seems to me that there are two broad types of kinaesthetic image operating here, with an intermediate third between these two. There are images of movement which seem to be mainly visual: as in 'blow' and 'laid'. Then there are images of *felt* movement (which in this poem dominate the composition): 'caressed', 'loosening', and 'shudder' are examples among others. Intermediate images seem to contain implications both of observed and felt movement: 'staggering' contains both possibilities, it seems to me. Others, which I have not marked, might also arguably belong in this category: such as 'terrified vague', which relates to 'push' and suggests qualities of movement which might be both internal and externally-witnessed.

I certainly would not insist upon the rightness of the assignments I have made to each notional category of kinaesthetic image. What I am directing attention to — what such an activity directs the students' attention to — is the preponderance of images of movement. Movement observed should, perhaps more strictly, be assigned to the visual sense-impression; except that there is an internal and corresponding sensation, which one may experience (such as, when one sees a child fall over, one may experience a sympathetic nervous sensation). In any case the categories of image would be dispersed in the ensuing discussion; they enable appreciation to proceed from apprehension to comprehension. What I would say *is* significant, however, is that collectively these images point most certainly to the sense of movement itself, a repertoire of mental images from which the poem generates its own momentum. Additionally, they point to the internal organization, the network of references which connects and makes correspondences across the space of the poem. One sees through this kind of scrutiny, for instance, how 'holds helpless' (which is the full form of the image) is gathered and summated by 'mastered' — the convergence to which other images are directed too.

'Leda and the Swan' collects the intense, cumulative force of sensation itself. It is especially, I would argue, in its access to images of internal kinaesthesis (almost literally 'muscle-sense') that the power and the potency of this great poem reside. They somehow embody, make sensate, the idea (the punless 'conception') of the poem, translating the abstract into the immediate. It is these images which foreshorten the distance between reader and event. Without them the poem would project the neutrality of the removed and disengaged observer.

Imagination and the Re-presentation of Experience

Memory images put the past to the service of the present, and in the context of the composition of a poem, contribute significantly to its emerging identity. Because, in the perception of immediate experience, we do not operate sense modes separately, or sequentially, but in the oneness of the fleeting moment, the representation of experience may combine recollects of different sense-impressions. Collectively they enforce a more intense realization — an integration of features of experience through which the unity of the poem is perceived. Such an assemblage of images within the confined location of a poem, for example, is an attendance to evidences of sense usually ignored or bypassed in the exigencies of any passing moment. Since we can not attend to them all, we must select. We direct our priorities within each moment of contending obligations. But when recollected in an exercise of memory which can potentially borrow features freely from the totality of all personal experience, then we are liberated to explore and to make awarenesses of what had hitherto gone unregarded. In this way memory images, recollects of the 'not here not now' actually expand the cognizable frame of reference of what we can attend to. The expression of these sensory images enables us thereby to develop a more inclusive and integrated sense of being. A poem — and by extension other literary forms and other arts — can make an organization of sense-impression from memory which is simply not available in the moment of perception itself. The poem makes apprehensible experience which would otherwise remain partial.

Sometimes, in the making of awareness, images transpose or combine the senses so as to produce a special case of synaesthesia. In a part of T.S. Eliot's 'The Love Song of J. Alfred Prufrock' (1917), for example, what is, to the observer, essentially a visual experience, is represented in the images of a kinaesthetic sense mode:

> The yellow fog that rubs its back upon the window-panes,
> The yellow smoke that rubs its muzzle on the window-panes,
> Licked its tongue into the corners of the evening,
> Lingered upon the pools that stand in drains,
> Let fall upon its back the soot that falls from chimneys,
> Slipped by the terrace, made a sudden leap,
> And seeing that it was a soft October night,
> Curled once about the house and fell asleep.[9]

Where recollects of past sense-impressions are combined across different sense modes a new perception is generated. Here, the images work concertedly to *animate*, quite literally, the perception. The fog is no longer simply a manifest 'observation'. What is seen has been reconstituted via images of movement. These then implicate the notions of stealth, of an animal and threatening presence.

The coordination, the arranging and interpenetration of images mark, as in Coleridge's formulation, the active agency of Imagination itself. From their origin in remembered experience sense-impressions are gathered and incorporated. Stephen Spender, in the same article (1946) from which I have previously quoted, presented the general outline in these terms:

> It is perhaps true to say that memory is the faculty of poetry, because imagination is itself an exercise of memory. There is nothing we imagine which we do not already know. And our ability to imagine is our ability to remember what we have experienced and to apply it to some different situation. Thus the greatest poets are those with memories so great that they extend beyond their strongest experiences to their minutest observations of people and things far outside their own self-centredness ...[10]

'There is nothing we imagine which we do not already know': here Spender both confirms the encounter of memory with the making of a poem (or any other art product, I have argued) and affirms the recognition made three centuries previously by Thomas Hobbes. In *Leviathan* (1651) Hobbes had written: 'There is no conception in a man's mind, which hath not at first, totally or by parts, been begotten upon the organs of sense.' Products of the imagination, the reminder serves to tell us, are in this way composited out of elements of past experience. There is a further dimension, one which Spender himself goes on to state: that the recombination in novel ways of these elements of past experience can thereby be fashioned according to circumstances outside of the literal experience of the poet or artist. These are 'imagined' projections: imagined in the sense of invention. A complex illustration of these matters is provided by the poem from which I diverged, T.S. Eliot's 'Prufrock'.

Eliot's poem is in the shape of a memory assembled out of selected passages of the history of the narrator, Prufrock. The memories are carried, in the main, by Prufrock's strongly-etched sense-impressions, together with invented imaginings. Neither Prufrock nor his memories should be seen in any simple sense as a correlate to, persona of, or substitute for, the composer — T.S. Eliot. (The general issue of the identification of an author's works in strictly autobiographical terms is taken up in Chapter 9).

The re-created memory of Prufrock we discover to be intensely visual; there are detailed recollects of his experience which proceed from an acute observation, as he reveals to readers of his snapshotted memoirs. He has also a well-developed aural sensitivity ('voices', 'music', 'mermaids singing' ...). There are images of taste ('Do I dare to eat a peach?') and of smell ('Is it perfume from a dress ...?'). Observed movement is detailed. But of the direct sensori-motor experience of touch there is little, if anything at all. Touch is, or at least certainly can be, the most intimate of all the senses; and it is from *this* sense experience that Prufrock is disenfranchised. Where Prufrock does break through into images of any kind of bodily experience, they are hypothetical and abstract, not remembered. They are intimidating, even threatening (as in 'sprawling on a pin,/When I am pinned and wriggling on the wall ...'). Because he will risk nothing ('Do I dare?'), he condemns himself to endless repetition; all that is known is all that will be known. Prufrock's escape from this cyclic repeat, and the only sensual experience he can contemplate with pleasure, is in the fantasy images of the mermaids — themselves posing no sexual threat they are signs of an impossible longing. Prufrock has brought to mind the fantasy images which bespeak the reality of his experience, but he will not engage with them ('I do not think they will sing to me'), and thus he will not recognize their import.

It is not the place here to carry through a detailed exegesis of the poem; my purpose is to show only that the 'memory' of Prufrock has been carefully constructed, whether intuitively, or with deliberation so designed by Eliot, is beside the point. Within the scheme and scope of that memory the sense-impressions available to Prufrock effect important perceptions which we make of his essential character, and hence the poem. From the encounter with the reality of *his* experience Prufrock turns aside. His encounter with memory provides all the evidence he requires in order to know the reality of his experience. It is there, implicit in what he says. At each point of potential recognition Prufrock turns aside — retreating, instead, into fantasy and whimsy.

Versions from the Past: Perspectives on the Present

Images of sense-impression are vital carriers of meaning in poetry, as they may be also in the novel and the short story. They provide sensuous and immediate connections by which we may engage not with *texte* but with the experience contained in the poem. They provide an access of directly sensuous apprehension. Sensation itself is unmediated experience. Perception is what we *make* of what we see (hear, touch, taste, smell, feel kinaesthetical- ly); perception shapes sensation to its images so that sense can begin to be made. Poetry which collects sense-impression thereby gives us meaning, or a potential-for-meaning which has immediacy; that immediacy to which Archibald MacLeish pointed, in *Poetry and Experience* (1961), when he wrote that the poet 'undertakes to "know" the world not by exegesis or demonstra- tion or proofs but directly, as a man knows apple in the mouth.'

Though Philip Larkin would appear subsequently to have regretted making that testament to his own poetic procedures gathered in D.J. En- right's *Poets of the 1950s* (1956), there is a part of that account which seems to me to have an especial validity. Endlessly quoted, it contains an insight easily overlooked because of the very familiarity of the expression:

> I write poems to preserve things ... both for myself and others, though I feel that my prime responsibility is to the experience itself, which I am trying to keep from oblivion for its own sake. Why I should do this I have no idea, but I think the impulse to preserve lies at the bottom of all art.[11]

'The experience itself' records that impersonalization of experience, the subjective/objective dissolve to which I directed attention in the previous chapter. 'The impulse to preserve' is the human counter to the fact of mortality; and what is being preserved is memory. Without memory a person has no identity.

Hence the cast of the poetic mind is necessarily rearward; rearward in the sense identified by Spender, and confirmed by T.S. Eliot:

> The poet's mind is in fact a receptacle for storing up numberless feelings, phrases, images, which remain there until all the particles which can unite to form a new compound are present together.[12]

Thus the 'history' recorded in a poem is memory played out in the present. It is a drama which enacts, rather than simply represents, its past: it is history-in-motion, on its way to being, seen in the perspective of events as they occur — an interplay of now and then, past and present. It is a history in which the duration of the occasion, and all which is recollected prompted by the occasion, are simultaneously co-active. Thus is the lyric poem almost bound to be 'occasional'; its concentration is the movement of mind within, around, and upon the moment of its impulse.

So a poem confronts us with a memory made immediate and full. It is coherent and united in a way which only the past, a version of the past, can be. The same, I would argue, is true of the novel — a form employing the discursive as well as the lyric, an extensive exercise with, prospectively, a variety of points of view[13] as against the singular perspective of the lyric poem. But the cast of mind in the making of the novel is rearward, too. The novel in its own ways offers us perspectives on 'history'; it is an exploration of what memory has reconstructed as its events, characters, descriptions, exchanges. It is history made interior — the subjective extension of self into those details of which it is composed, informed by the intention to understand. It is not history as a record merely — a fact brilliantly realized in Norman Mailer's *Armies of the Night* (1968), a work in two Books: 'History as a Novel', and 'The Novel as History'. Here, in the recounting of the massed protest of anti-Vietnam War demonstrators, who marched upon the Pentagon in October 1967, Mailer arrives in his telling at 'the front line, at the six inches of no-man's-land across which troops and demonstrators — in the closest use yet of this word — confront each other'. At this point of his narrative, where demonstrators stand on the guarded Pentagon steps, Mailer offers the following reflection:

> . . . the first book can be, in the formal sense, nothing but a personal history which while written as a novel was to the best of the author's memory scrupulous to facts, and therefore a document: whereas the second, while dutiful to all newspaper accounts, eyewitness reports, and historic inductions available . . . is finally now to be disclosed as some sort of condensation of a collective novel . . . [14]

The historian's pretence of distanced objectivity, of narrating events as detached from the experience of those who compose the history, has to be abandoned. The reasons for this, in Mailer's words, reduce to one:

> . . . an explanation of the mystery of the events at the Pentagon cannot be developed by the methods of history — only by the instincts of the novelist . . . the difficulty is that the history is interior — no documents can give sufficient information: the novel must replace history at precisely that point where experience is sufficiently emotional, spiritual, psychical, moral, existential, or supernatural to expose the fact that the historian in pursuing the experience would be obliged to quit the clearly demarcated limits of historic inquiry.[15]

All the histories of literature are interior in the sense identified by Mailer — whether in poetry or in novel form. Novelists, whether engaging with historic fact, as Mailer, or with the potential world of experience liberated by a persistent image, as John Fowles (see chapter 6), or with the imaginative reconstruction of a society, as George Eliot in *Middlemarch* (1871–2), all attempt to get to the *reality* of that *experience*, rather than the recording of fact. It is the narration of this special kind of gathering of recalled experience which makes works of art interior histories. Only through such living intimacy can the human condition be known.

Thus literary works are those special histories supercharged with a sense of the present, as they were in their composition, and as they are in our reading of them, if we cooperate with the text to reanimate experience. Predominantly, in poetry, this immediacy is generated out of recollects of sensory impression put to a present service. Such images mediate, and perhaps even realize, whatever thought, idea, attitude and feeling might have been the initial impulse to the gathering of experience which becomes the poem. The novel too, in its more extensive space, works through sense-impression to get as close as possible to the representation of those realities towards which it is directed. In this way literary writings, which are recompositions of history, become the enforcers of the immediate. For they construct a mode of history with which we can engage with an immediacy of apprehension and the fulness of our senses: a mode of history which is not simply the recording or recalling of past event, but a sense of history which *is being experienced* (the illusion of the present in the tense of lyric poetry), or a sense of history *as experienced*, in the case of the novel.

Notes and References

1 Warnock, M. (1976) *Imagination*, London, Faber and Faber, p. 194.
2 Harding, R.E. (1948) *An Anatomy of Inspiration and an Essay on the Creative Mood*, 3rd edn., Cambridge, Heffer.
3 Hope, A.D. (1979) *The New Cratylus*, Oxford, Oxford University Press, p. 64.
4 Spender, S. (1946) 'The Making of a Poem', *Partisan Review*, 13, p. 302.
5 Still one of the most productive sources for an exploration of the psychology of mental images and their application to art works (as well as other psychological 'conditions'), I would here recommend McKellar, P. (1957) *Imagination and Thinking*, London, Cohen and West.
6 Eliot, T.S. (1933) 'The Use of Poetry and the Use of Criticism', in Hayward, J. (Ed.) (1963) *Selected Prose*, London, Peregrine, pp. 89–90.
7 Thomas, R.G. (Ed.) (1978) *The Collected Poems of Edward Thomas*, Oxford, Oxford University Press, pp. 19–20.
8 Yeats, W.B. (1965) *The Collected Poems*, London, Macmillan, p. 241.
9 Eliot, T.S. (1969) *The Complete Poems and Plays of T.S. Eliot*, London, Faber and Faber, p. 13.
10 Spender, *op. cit.*, p. 304.
11 Enright, D.J. (Ed.) (1956) *Poets of the 1950s*, Tokyo, Kenkyusha, p. 77.
12 Eliot, T.S. (1919) 'Tradition and the Individual Talent', *Selected Prose*, *op. cit.*, p. 27.
13 Detailed most extensively by Booth, W. (1961) *The Rhetoric of Fiction*, Chicago, University of Chicago Press.
14 Mailer, N. (1968) *The Armies of the Night*, London, Weidenfeld and Nicholson, p. 255.
15 *Ibid.*

Chapter 3

Symbolic Form, Tradition, Culture

No poet, no artist of any sort, has
his complete meaning alone. His significance,
his appreciation is the appreciation of his
relation to the dead poets and artists... I mean
this as a principle of aesthetic, not merely
historical, criticism.

T.S. Eliot[1]

Form: the Organization of Experience

In the encounter with the reality of experience the artist attempts to give
shape to the significance of that world. The encounter therefore necessarily
engages the artist with matters of *form*, since that which is formless subsists
without definition in the flux of experience. Form is essential if things are to
be brought into being. Simply in the shaping of experience — finding some
means by which experience can be represented — a kind of intelligence is
added. That intelligence, as previously outlined, binds knower and known in
an order of reality neither exclusively objective nor subjective. This understanding of the composition of realities, especially as they can be devised and
shared within a culture, is essential if societies are to comprehend each other.
It is the basis of the thesis made by Louis J. Halle in his discussion of
international relations:

> We understand nothing, our minds admit nothing, except in terms
> of some conceptual order. When we see a great light rise regularly on
> the eastern horizon, cross the sky, and disappear below the western
> horizon, we are drawn as conscious beings to find or devise an
> explanation, to evoke an order in the mind that will account for the
> phenomenon. We can no more avoid doing this than we can make
> our minds blank, excluding all images, notions, or thoughts. We are
> bound to supply ourselves at least with some tacit, unformulated
> explanation of the existential phenomenon, an explanation which

represents the conceptual world. We may adopt, by way of explanation, the concept of a sun god; or we may adopt the concept of a fiery mass about which our planet revolves while spinning on its own axis. In any case, we can think of the existential phenomenon at all only in terms of a conceptual order that our minds impose on it.[2]

Form is order. Order is not something super-added to that which one is attempting to do in art; a 'shape', as it were, which one grafts onto or imposes upon a piece. Form is the indispensable means by which the realization proceeds. Without form there is no making and nothing can be made. Form is not a quality or property 'given' to the artwork after-the-event of its conceptualization; it is the forming itself, it is the bringing-into-being. It is the organizing of experience.

Thus the artistic encounter with the reality of experience is a demand (however tacitly or implicitly known in the time of making) for form which will accommodate the impulse to the creation of the artwork. Form defines that initial impulse; or, more accurately, the experimentation with form will define the impulse. Form enables the making to proceed, however provisionally, and however the evolving shape of the piece will change, and be recast or revised in the making. Form should not be taken of necessity to imply a strict geometry, a traditional and defined shape to which the experience-being-explored *must* conform. Form here implies a patterning by which the experience may be known at all. And this is so even if, in the event, the art-product does achieve a distinctively recognizable form for which, through tradition, we have a conventional description; a sonnet or fugue, for example. The paradox of art-making is that form not only contains the experience, as a receptacle, but that the experience is itself shaped by the form. The search for appropriate form is a vital part of the inquiry into the status and meaning of experience.

The encounter with the need for form engages with the art-in-progress. Experience itself demands patterning, if it is to move towards any kind of meaning. The urge towards meaning imposes the demand for a shaping which will most fittingly realize the experience. Without such a patterning experience cannot achieve articulation. It may be, on occasion, that the form of the eventual piece is seen *a priori*, its justness 'seen' clearly in advance of the composing. Somehow the reality of experience and a shape for its projection have occurred simultaneously, even spontaneously. The work emerges 'ready-made'. On most other occasions the eventual form of the piece will be far less certainly perceived; what is to be presented and the manner of its presentation are intimately connected in the exploration of the projected work.

Culture and the Traditions of Form

The engagement with the need for form and the emergence of that form involve us, therefore, in an encounter both with *culture* and *medium*. These too have a reciprocal relationship within the matrix of the artistic endeavour.

The notion of culture is fraught with difficulties of definition — in the stylized language of intellectual debate today, is 'problematic'. In his classic work on *Culture and Society 1780–1950* (1958) Raymond Williams traced the evolution of meanings applied to the term.[3] Before the eighteenth century culture was equated with the 'tending of natural growth'. In the eighteenth and early nineteenth centuries the word became separated from its association with (our present sense of) 'cultivation' to stand in its own right as a thing apart. The meaning of culture then passed through that of 'a general state or habit of the mind' to 'the general state of intellectual development in a society as a whole'. Later still culture came to stand for 'the general body of the arts', and then enlarged its reference to mean 'a whole way of life, material, intellectual and spiritual'. In the context of the arts, culture refers us to the accumulated history of the aesthetic activity of a society. But that history should be seen as active, with a potential for action, as other associations attaching to culture also enable us to see. For culture does refer to the notion of natural growth, of art-making as a natural extension of human biology — culture as 'the completion of instinct'.[4] In this sense it has affinities with that personal history, memory, encountered in the creative act. Culture, because its artistic artefacts can enter into personal memory and influence personality, may be reanimated with each fresh creation.

And each fresh creation does, to some degree — whether contrived or merely by implication — invoke previous artefacts. A novel invokes notions of novel, every new novel imprinting itself upon, and sometimes against, the impression of previous novels. From time to time an artist, or a group of artists, emerges whose own practice and new art-forms question the validity of the conventions of current or past practice. Thus are born those movements in art, sometimes loosely-held affinities among a group of practitioners, sometimes clearly-defined as manifestos, which react against existing forms. It is not without significance that such movements do so define themselves against the history of the art, or selected periods of the art (usually the immediately preceding period), and almost always with an insistence that those forms to be rejected somehow pervert the nature of the 'new' reality which the contemporary practitioners are seeking to express. What binds all such movements, no matter to which period of history they refer, is a certain sense that a particular form has become superannuated as a means of representing *contemporary* history. After all, a culture in which no new forms were possible would be one condemned to an endless replication of its existing forms, copy after copy, until they became mindless clones, what they symbolized no longer apprehended by their makers.

Thus, even in the extreme case where the heritage of practice is rejected, art works, in whatever medium, owe something to previous works in that medium. One recalls the remark of Ernst Gombrich: 'All pictures owe more to previous pictures than to nature.'

There is a truth here which one can readily acknowledge, the influence of previous works upon any present undertaking. It is a truth to be qualified, the degree of indebtedness of any one work to previous works; there are, after all, the so-called 'primitive' painters, some of whom have limited knowledge of and acquaintanceship with previous forms. Substantial knowledge, in the academic sense, may not be what is required; the knowledge can be small, but intimate and personal. Some artists do not require — for the realization of *their* versions of reality, their vision — extensive acquaintance-ship with a diversity of forms. It may be that what is required is a continual refinement of a given form.

All art owes *something* (more or less) to previous art — from which it might be tempting to see each work of art as an attenuation of previous art, each sample becoming more of an artifice, and the whole of art becoming an elaborate artificiality. Art would thus somehow *oppose* nature, since art would merely comment on art, not on life. There is a contrary view, one which sees the nature of man extending itself quite naturally into the pro-duction of art, — of art as the continuing evolution of man's inherent nature — and the means by which we come into conscious awareness of what that nature is. Culture, in the sense of the aesthetic products of that awareness, would then be the natural outgrowth of this evolving self-awareness.

Or are artworks merely the 'playthings' which Freud believed them to be — the occupations of time with which mankind became involved once the demands of physical survival had been satisfied? Such a view is certainly refuted in the findings of anthropologists. The example of cave paintings and other artefacts produced by 'primitive' societies, whose physical survival was by no means certain, would appear to testify against the notion. Of course, there may well be a sense of play involved in artmaking, in certain works prominently and deliberately displayed, just as there may be intellectual play involved — that 'puzzle interest' of poetry, for example. There is no neces-sary contradiction between playfulness and seriousness; the 'serious play' of art achieves its many forms by which personal experience may be known. Each form, referencing to some degree previous works, is thereby a 'history' both personal and cultural, borrowing from the artistic forms of a culture as a means of exploring and defining the personal. In the long accumulation of example which composes the culture of art-forms many of those which started as an act of formal rebellion against the inherited forms will them-selves be incorporated, becoming part of the culture, in the passage of time.

Personal Impulse and the Autonomy of Form

The culture offers its diversity of forms. It is to be expected that practitioners of any art would seek to learn from precedent. For that history, which provides the culture, continues to offer a rich and varied resource of examples and models within and through which one may move towards personal articulation. Once completed, the particular artwork records the history of the artist's encounter with

> Already lived experience
> Through a convention that creates
> Autonomous completed states.

> W.H. Auden: from *New Year Letter*, 1940)[5]

The 'autonomy' of the 'completed state' of the work means that it has achieved its own identity. It may to greater or lesser extent satisfactorily realize the artist's ambition to make sense of lived experience. Whatever the degree of success of the realization, it is important not to overlook the personal drive towards a making of sense. To whatever extent the work of art borrows from, or reacts against, the precedents held within the culture, the personal impulse of the artist remains. The notion of the Intentionalist Fallacy reminds us of the fact that the meaning which results from an artwork may well vary from that which the artist had conceived. The artist cannot have full authority over the determination of what her or his work signifies, simply because of the range of perspectives from which the reader, listener, or viewer, attends to the art. There is the added fact that the work itself may employ implicatory systems of meaning of which the artist was personally unaware; signs, if you prefer, with multiple possible significations. A work may mean more or less than, or something different from, that which the maker intended or had consciously perceived or conceived. It is a fact which even that artist who had most consciously attended to the work-in-the-making must acknowledge. It is acknowledged, for example, in the afterthoughts of William Golding reflecting upon *Lord of the Flies* (1954):

> May it not be that at the very moments when I felt the fable come to its own life before me it may in fact have become something more valuable, so that where I thought it was failing, it was really succeeding? I leave that consideration to the many learned and devoted persons, who in speech and the printed word, have explained to me what the story means. For I have shifted somewhat from the position I held when I wrote the book. I no longer believe that the author has a kind of *patria potestas* over his brainchildren. Once they are printed they have reached their majority and the author has no more authority over them, knows no more about them, perhaps knows less about them than the critic who comes fresh to them, and sees them not as the author hoped they would be, but as what they are.[6]

The discoveries, those 'epiphanies' to which A.D. Hope referred, which an artist makes about her or his work, continue even after the completion of the work itself. The knowledge cannot be known until the work is finished, and when finished, the network of symbolization of which it is composed achieves its own reference system. In part, the autonomy of a finished work of art derives its independence from its association with other works. David Lodge in his essay 'Modernism, Antimodernism and Postmodernism' (1978) characterized an extension of the argument in the following way:

> 'Life imitates art', declared Oscar Wilde, meaning that we compose the reality we perceive by mental structures that are cultural, not natural in origin, and that it is art which is most likely to change and renew those structures when they become inadequate or unsatisfying. 'Where, if not from the Impressionists', he asked, 'do we get those wonderful brown fogs that come creeping down our streets, blurring the gaslamps and changing the houses into monstrous shadows?'
> But if life imitates art, where does art come from? The answer

given is: from other art, especially art of the same kind. Poems are not made out of experience, they are made out of poetry — that is, the tradition of disposing the possibilities of language to poetic ends — modified, to be sure, by the particular experience of the individual poet, but in no straightforward sense an expression of it.[7]

Did Eliot, one wonders, get *his* fog (in the lines I have quoted previously from *Prufrock*) from the Impressionists? or from Oscar Wilde? or from direct experience? And where, to complicate matters, did Dickens get *this* fog?

Fog everywhere. Fog up the river, where it flows among green aits and meadows; fog down the river, where it rolls defiled among the tiers of shipping, and the waterside pollutions of a great (and dirty) city . . .[8]

At the time of Oscar Wilde's mock-serious comments, (in *Imitations*, 1891), the Impressionists' work of the 1860s onwards had become widely known. Dickens's *Bleak House* was serialized in 1852–3. In one sense, of course, it does not matter at all — within the particular artwork itself — where the fog comes from. It may come from other works; it may spring from direct experience, as it surely did in the case of Dickens. What *does* matter is the use to which the fog is put in any given example — not the fact of the fog, but the purpose it serves, the metaphorical implications to which it points. The way in which the materials of art may be deployed refers us again to the culture of those structures, for there we learn the systems of organization which we may repeat, amend, or attempt to destroy.

Beneath the surface play of Wilde's remarks, an important observation emerges. It is in the recognition that art may very well enable us to form new perceptions of reality and new ways of conceiving that composition of our individual and social beings which we call reality. That, arguably, is the supreme function of art — an argument to be supported in the means by which art fashions a sense of reality; a means which engages the whole psyche in the fashioning of the work — one which is not exclusively intellectual. The possessions of experience necessarily include, therefore, one's memory of other works of art and their effects. They too are a part of the reality of experience. The distinction between art as an issue from direct experience and as an issue out of other art misses a simple, but essential fact: the relationship which exists between the two. The work of art occupies a space which is not, as it were, *alongside*, experience. It is an integral part of experience. To acknowledge that artworks may borrow significantly from other examples within the culture should not be seen to dispossess the artist of personal impulse, the first impulse to make sense, however provisionally, of a sensed reality.

Lodge's formulation that poems 'are made out of poetry — that is, the tradition of disposing the possibilities of language to poetic ends, modified, to be sure, by the particular experience of the individual poet, but in no straightforward sense an expression of it' — is one recognition of the importance of the tradition of cultural forms. The extent to which, in any one work, that cultural tradition gives shape to the new composition will vary from artist to artist, from work to work. For culture is not inert. It is not simply an accumulation of facts *about* a history of cultural forms (though it can be presented as such in an academic exercise). Culture is an accumulated response to a succession of endeavours to make sense of the fact of living. It is a sensibility, a way of perceiving reality. As the conditions for one's living change through the movement of personal, social, and political history, the realities which they bespeak may alter too. Some works, some artists, may thereby become discredited; they no longer connect with the contemporary sense of reality — however large their reputation in their own times. Others may be rediscovered in later times. This, in brief, is what we mean by significance. It is relatedness, a significance which can be argued from both a contemporary and a historical perspective. But whatever choices one makes, the whole movement of the culture remains. That is the recognition which Eliot made in his essay of 1919, 'Tradition and the Individual Talent'.

Eliot's essay, a *locus classicus* of modern criticism, is an argument ultimately for the impersonality of the completed work of art. No matter how personal or uniquely autobiographical in the origins of the impelling experience, generating the impulse to create, the final product will be a sublimation or diffusion of the esoteric. At the very least it will be dissolved, to greater or lesser extent, in the solution of history — that special history which Eliot meant by tradition:

> [Tradition] cannot be inherited, and if you want it you must obtain it by great labour. It involves, in the first place, the historical sense, which we may call nearly indispensable to anyone who would continue to be a poet beyond his twenty-fifth year; and the historical sense involves a perception, not only of the pastness of the past, but of its presence; the historical sense compels a man to write not merely with his own generation in his bones, but with a feeling that the whole of the literature of Europe from Homer and within it the whole of the literature of his own country has a simultaneous existence and composes a simultaneous order ...[9]

Eliot's advocacy is a rationalization of his own poetic enterprise, and one must approach it with caution. Not all poets, not all artists, start from or go on to adopt the prescription as he has delineated it. Nonetheless, tradition, the history of culture, is something with which one actively engages. It is a participation *now* which both shapes and alters one's mode of perception, one's thoughts and feelings. Such involvement in the tradition makes possible a greater sense of being, a fuller representation of self within history. Culture, in the sense in which Eliot writes of it *enables the individual to complete her or his identity*, whilst at the same time enlarging the frame of reference. It is a dynamic, not a social possession with which to show off at cocktail parties or to leave lying around on coffee tables. For in the end one can not define self autistically: nor can artists so construct their works *ex nihilo*. Each work of art connects with the culture, and to the extent that each work of art is grounded in and tested against the tradition of that culture, so is the work itself in some degree impersonal. What I mean by impersonal, and what I believe Eliot meant here, is that — *seen within the culture* — a work of art can stand on its own; it does not require biographical glosses in order to make sense. Seen within the culture the work acquires an order of referencing by which it may be approached, its own distinctive form enabling us to see its own distinctiveness.

Exploring the Tradition

Tradition, strictly, refers to the handing on of the culture, from generation to generation. In one sense — the sense invariably adopted by its detractors and denigrators — it is almost unavoidably the case that tradition will be conservative. That which a tradition will most easily and readily assimilate will be that which is most like the tradition — more of the same. But similar is not identical, a mimed repetition. Even within a conservative cultural tradition there will be a wide variety of forms, and a potential for combining elements from the tradition which, potentially, will serve always to revitalize the tradition (as well as enforce it). It is a kind of Rebel and Establishment conversion. That which opposed, even sought to destroy the tradition, becomes a part of that tradition — as has Eliot himself.

Yet for the artist the prior forms of the art remain as significant means for the exploration of the personal within the cultural medium — whether or not one accepts the ideology of the particular artist. Poets who would reject entirely Eliot's stated social, political, and religious views have nonetheless learned from his *poetry* some of the principles by which they can proceed in their own compositions. For when we examine the notion of form within any of the artistic traditions of a culture, whether those of literature, dance, drama, music, film, or the visual arts, what we discover are the significant modes of symbolization by which the successive generations of that culture have attempted to come to terms with the shifting variety of experience.

Indeed, the reality is that personal expression becomes possible only *because of* and *through* the existence of these symbolic forms. Without a symbolic system of some kind it simply would not be possible to make the realizations which one has. To think, to conceive, demands some symbolic means by which to conduct such a processing of experience. There must be a medium by which symbolically to transform experience, and there must be a form within which the medium is capable of expression. It is the extent to which these symbolic languages and their forms are shared, their conventions understood, which makes possible, additionally, the fact of communication among and between persons. The history of a culture reveals to us the ways in which the systems of symbolization have been employed in the past and suggests to us possibilities both for renewal of those forms and for the improvisation of new structures through a combination of previously used elements. The culture offers the structural properties of form, actualized examples of the ways in which the medium has been deployed. Understanding their principles, the shaping of historic forms and their purposes, is what I would wish to see as the tradition of education *into* the arts. Such an aesthetic induction would enable us to perceive networks of potential relationships, the expressive possibilities of the history of the culture.

Defining the culture confronts us, of course, with massive difficulties.

Yet, without an induction into the formal properties of a culture, I do not see how one can conduct an education into the arts. I write this the day after my involvement, with two fellow practitioners, in an Arts Day at a secondary school in which we worked participatively with fourth and fifth year pupils to produce words and music presentations. What became clear, to all three of us, was that the pupils were locked within the contemporary — and within a very narrow band of the contemporary at that. Music was pop music, or rather a small sample of the great variety of forms which are all lumped together under the unsatisfactory label of pop music. Poetry was the words sung against the simplest of repetitive rhythms. It did not matter much what the words were; they provided the voice with something to do. I hope I shall not be misunderstood, though I expect to be charged with élitism. I can only assert that this is not an argument against popular music — far from it. I listen a great deal to it, I enjoy much of it, and I have worked (and do work) with musicians in that field, to my own great benefit. There is much pop music which is manufactured, a cliché of platitude, both in words and in musical terms — music which is designed to fit a defined slot in a record company's scheme of merchandising; that is true. But there is also authentic popular music, and popular musical forms can be as valid as any other forms of music for the realization of experience.[10] Those musicians I work with have, first, an extensive *working knowledge* of the great variety of form within which popular music can operate — blues, rock, jazz, reggae, and so on — and a developed understanding of a great many other musical traditions, including what is loosely called the 'classical'. They know too and have a great interest in popular music which borrows freely from other music from around the world. The musical traditions of diverse societies — African, Afro-Caribbean, Indian, South American — can suggest alternative formal properties which, for their own distinct purposes, they on occasion incorporate into their own work.

The pupils' limited experience of music, however, was matched by their lack of understanding of literary form. The pupils I worked with had little acquaintance with the formal properties of poetry or story — the two modes within which we were creating their works, exploring, experimenting, and improvising what would become a performed presentation at the end of that day's work. Two boys, for example, guitarists in their own pop group, wanted to compose words to go with a blues riff they had learned to play. Yet neither had any idea as to the formal requirements of the shape of the language required if, to put it very simply, it was to 'fit' the rhythmic organization. In the end I offered them make-do words, of no originality, to demonstrate the formal organization of words required. Then they were *free to compose their own words on the theme they had in mind.* They had no understanding of the tradition within which they had chosen to work. Similarly, a group of five pupils, four girls and a boy, had no understanding of the formal properties of narrative within which to make their production on their chosen theme, nightmare — though through one of our sessions they had accumulated, by a sharing of experience, all the images required for the composition and had begun to explore the qualities of nightmare experience held in common. But they did not know how to *tell* (not at all the same thing as to *write*) a story. In this instance, by experimenting with musical sounds on a range of instruments, they began to see how to organize the telling; the music enabling them to leave much unsaid, as it were. They also discovered, through rehearsal, the pauses, pace, and tones of voice required in the oral art-form of telling a story. The discovery, obvious to readers of this book, that the telling of a particular story, as in their case, demanded two voices — so that thematically the voices could play off each other — was for them a possibility they had not previously encountered.

Only through an encounter with the cultural forms of the past can we be liberated, artistically, from the tyranny of the present. Lacking that, we are condemned to a perception of the contemporary springing, ready-made, from the stuff of its own self, with no reference beyond its own time. Lacking the possibility of renewal it must feed upon itself until exhausted.

Extending the Tradition

Just as an artistic form draws upon sources within the cultural history, so may a culture look to other cultures for renewal, growth, and inspiration. A major difficulty we have with any attempt to define a tradition is that all such attempts must be partial and exclusive. The tradition becomes a selection from the tradition. The formulation of the Great Tradition in English literature (1948), as made by the influential critic F.R. Leavis, has brought forth objections at several levels. At one level, objections have concentrated upon the sins of omissions, rather than a flat rejection of (some or all) of Leavis's selected works.[11] At another level, the objections made are against the presumption that only a small and educated élite has the power of trained discrimination by which to establish which works are of substance and value and which are merely meretricious; *who* is entitled to define the tradition replaces the argument about *what* that tradition is. There is, too, a social objection one can bring to such a listing — that it concentrates upon the national characteristics of its works rather than the cultural.

Chaucer, Shakespeare, and countless other writers *in* English (the medium) have drawn their sources and their inspirations from other cultures; they have drawn them from the European tradition to which Eliot referred. In translation or in their original tongues, other writers have drawn and do draw additionally from non-European sources. English is also the language of composition for writers from other societies — African, Indian, and Afro-Caribbean, for example. The literary products of the cultures of other societies are also available through the art of translation into English. The potential *field* for engagement with literature is far wider than that implied in the national traditions of British literature. Any investigation into the place of literature in education is bound, I believe, to consider these implications. For there are sound educational reasons why we should perhaps begin to look to what I have called the field of literature in this way rather than commit ourselves to national samples only.

First, we live in a multi-cultural society. Education must not merely accept the fact but actively engage with the fact. A culture is a part of one's inheritance. To deny that culture, even passively, is in some way to deny the reality of one's identity. Second, though in the encounter with literatures of different societies there may well be a sense of strangeness, that strangeness is not in itself an impenetrable barrier. For works of art operate as symbolic representations of reality, not as guide-books to actuality. We interact with them as metaphors: imaginative truths do not demand literal living for us to perceive their validity. Chinua Achebe's *Things Fall Apart* (1958) may present a picture of a remote society — remote historically even to Achebe himself, as he has said — but the imaginative truths which its narrative symbolizes can be immediately apprehended.[12] In this convergence of the human experience we begin to sense likenesses and demote differences. If nations cannot understand each other through their politicians, perhaps the redemption of art will at least enable us to share with each other.

Taking such a view enables us to honour the traditions of different societies or nations, whilst enlarging the frame of reference as to what may be admitted to the literary culture. The problem of selection would still remain, might indeed be even larger. But if we are to avoid arbitrary nomination, I should like to consider, first, the bases on which selection might be made. Within these I believe there would be no reduction in the scope for individual selection, but perhaps a greater certainty in the choices, both of individual works and in the educational programme to which they would contribute.

Working Within the Genres of Literary Form

It may be that certain kinds of experience achieve their most apposite realizations in certain mediums: the various 'languages' of the arts of literature, dance, music, drama, film, and the visual arts. These are very broad categories, many of which may borrow procedures and ideas from each other. Each of the arts contains subsets of examples, or species, which share significant features in common. These organizations of the art we may denote by the term genre: a classification by shape, intention, and methodology, through which we relate features held in common among and between individual works. Each genre deploys one or more modes of the language for the projection of experience, using the vocabulary, syntax, and symbols of that art category (literature, dance, etc.) in characteristic ways. Form, therefore, as the artistic realization of experience, employs its particular medium in distinctive ways. These are located within that communal possession we call culture. Culture in this sense, though not in the sociological sense, represents the history of preceding endeavours to use the medium to produce various art forms. Within culture resides the potential of its forms to realize new products, new representations of the reality of experience.

Within a literature programme, therefore, the notion of genre and the variety of modes of which it is composed, can provide a significant educational experience on two counts. First, acquaintance with and understanding of the genre enables critical discrimination to proceed more certainly. The likenesses and divergences of a particular work being examined may thereby be more positively established. Works of art can, and often do, play off other works of art within the same genre. An understanding of genre, to put it simply, helps us to see how a particular artwork 'works'. We develop insights into its making through a recognition of its formal properties, the conventions within which and by which it operates. Thus, we may more certainly approach its interpretation, the meanings which inhere. Second, the range of works within a genre provide significant points of departure for the students' personal endeavours to make art, to engage creatively with the reality of *their* experience. I do not believe that it is profitable for the student to attempt to *copy*, as model, a given example of a genre; that most often leads to a distortion of the original impulse to art-making from which the student begins. The authenticity of the experience will be distorted by the needs of too close an adherence to the formal properties of the given example — such as we witness when students follow slavishly a rhyme-scheme in a poem of their own making. The poem then ends up 'rhyming', true, but the piece as a whole is often inconsequential. There is a strong case, however, for an active experimentation with the formal properties of a genre; releasing students into their own creativity by encouraging them to employ selectively some of the possibilities of form. One must use to one's own purposes the possibilities of form, not rigidly replicate the details of any one particular example. But a knowledge of the formal properties of genre, a perception of the purposes they might serve, can provide a rich resource of means and devices *through which the particularity of personal experience can be articulated.* Additionally, of course, these elements of form *can* be transposed across different genres — a fact we can see in numberless experimentations with form.

Throughout the years of schooling, therefore, we might expect the student to be presented with opportunities for literary engagement across a wide variety of genres. Peter Abbs,[13] in a companion volume in this series of books, has previously indicated what such a range might include:

Poetry
Myth
Fairy tale
Novel
Story
Autobiography
Journal/diary
Letter
Memoir
Documentary
Scripted drama
Essay and Sketch
Rhetoric (public speech, polemic, etc.)

The list is intended to be indicative, not definitive. There is a complication: some of the genres are also particular modes of realization. Autobiography may be written in the mode of poetry or memoir, letter, drama, and others; story may be composed as letter(s), diary, documentary ... and so on. The purpose here is not to construct an elaborate taxonomy of Linnaean complexity (we should remember that Linnaeus himself went mad in the pursuit of his own system!), but to illustrate the diversity of form which may be shaped by the various uses of these modes within a genre. The possible complexities were recognised by Abbs himself, who goes on to give a working illustration of the modes which one genre, that of story, might entail:

Epistolary
Journal/diary
Documentary
Dialogue
First person narration
Second person narration
Third person narration
Stream of consciousness
Experimental

Again, there are matters here for discussion and probable elaboration, yet the notions of form and mode within genre undoubtedly offer a useful starting-point from which to explore the literary culture. At the very least they provide us with basic concepts by which to begin to delineate the rich variety of literary works. Potentially their explication will provide more than that, however. Notions of genre will guide our approach to literary works — to the students' own making, and to those re-creative activities of expressive criticism by which we engage with literary works. The formal properties of each genre, and the possibilities of their projection via a range of modes, will provide students with an indispensable guide to the reading of literature. Their reading will be an active experimentation with form, the traditions of genre and the aesthetic properties of each available mode providing a sharper perception of the unique form of the piece, its uniqueness now evident by what it shares with, and in what ways it differs from, other examples within the tradition of that form.

Making and Re-making Literary Form

A significant part of the exploration into the genres of literary culture should be through the students' active experimentation, the creating of their own works. Reading will inform making, and making will inform reading. Each procedure animates the other. In learning to make literature we learn how to read it; in reading literature we more certainly can learn how to compose it. A literary programme devised around a progressive investigation into samples of the forms of various genres would provide a rich resource for the location of personal experience, and a fund of opportunities for all the arts disciplines, not just literature, within an arts community.

Between what I have called, in shorthand, the reading of literature and the writing of literature, there is the possibility of a third expressive activity. This is creative transposition. Individually or collectively students transpose a literary work, or a part of that work, from its original genre to another — or from its given mode(s) to other mode(s). Transposition is in itself an interpretative act; without close attention to the original, transposition is not possible.

Innumerable transpositions are possible, setting varying degrees of complexity. A poem or story can be recast as a journal or diary record; two characters in a novel may correspond to each other about the events to which they are observers or events in which they are implic ted ... and so on. From a reading of short stories a group of my teachers-in-training went on to write their own short stories, of which one was selected to be transposed in.o the form of a radio play, which they were going to record. Immediately the conventions of scripting were encountered — the physical layout of type-script. More importantly, however, the differences between dialogue and naturalistic speech became very evident. As soon as the students had to *say* the words, some of the artificialities in the story's dialogue demanded rewriting. Unsupported by textual props, the commentary which narrative can supply to the dialogue, the language of the dialogue would no longer do. Such recognition led not only to rewriting, based now on orally trying out the shape of the words, but to a consideration of the role of the narrator, and to the place and purpose of sound effects (especially if these were to avoid cliché). After experimentation and rehearsal they then went into the cubicle which served as our sound recording studio. Further revisions then had to be made as the recording proceeded — including, I recall, considerable revisions of the projected timings for the drop-in of some of the sound effects. The potentials of each genre and various modes were explored within this extended creative enterprise. Sometimes limitations, too, are encountered — as when another group of students proved the uniqueness of form in Robert Graves's poem, 'Welsh Incident'[14] by attempting to transpose it into the style of a newspaper account.

*

The artistic encounter with experience encounters the need for form. Without form there is no making and nothing can be made. Form organizes experience; it is the means by which an artwork proceeds to its realization. In realizing that form, drawing upon the traditions and possibilities of the genres of culture and their modes of expression, experience is itself composited so that it may be recognized. A literary education founded on aesthetic principles looks both to the past and to the present of cultural forms, and to their potencies for expression, by which we may explore and come to terms with the contemporary and the personal.

Notes and References

1 Eliot, T.S. 'Tradition and the Individual Talent', in Hayward, J. (Ed.) (1963) *Selected Prose*, London, Peregrine, p. 23.

2 Halle, L.J. (1965) *The Society of Man*, London, Chatto and Windus, p. 37.

3 Williams, R. (1961) *Culture and Society 1780–1950*, Harmondsworth, Penguin, p. 16.

4 Midgley, M. (1979) *Beast and Man*, Harvester, quoted by Abbs, P. (1989) *A is for Aesthetic*, London, Falmer Press, p. 166.

5   Auden, W.H. (1974) *Collected Longer Poems*, London, Faber and Faber, p. 81.
6   Golding, W. (1965) 'Fable', in *The Hot Gates*, London, Faber and Faber, p. 100.
7   Lodge, D. (1981) *Working with Structuralism*, London, Routledge and Kegan Paul, p. 5.
8   Dickens, C. (1971) *Bleak House*, Harmondsworth, Penguin, p. 49.
9   Eliot, T.S., *op. cit.*, pp. 22–3.
10 For a detailed argument as to the contributions which pop music can make to musical education see Vulliamy, G.L. and Lee, E. (Eds) (1980) *Pop Music in School*, 2nd edn, Cambridge, Cambridge University Press.
11 Leavis, F.R. (1960) *The Great Tradition*, 2nd. edn., London, Chatto and Windus. The attacks upon Leavis's alleged élitism concentrate largely upon his work (1930) *Mass Civilisation and Minority Culture*, London, Chatto and Windus; reprinted as appendix III in Leavis, F.R. (1943) *Education and the University*, London, Chatto and Windus.
12 Achebe, C. (1958) *Things Fall Apart*, London, Heinemann.
13 Abbs, P. *A is for Aesthetic, op. cit.*, pp. 69–72.
14 Graves, R. (1975) *Collected Poems*, London, Cassell, pp. 71–2.

Chapter 4

Language: the Agent of Discovery

[The artist's] world is his language. What
it says to him it says about himself; his
imaginative vision of it is his self-knowledge...
The act of coming to know himself is the act
of converting his impressions into ideas, and so
of converting himself from mere psyche into
consciousness... Moreover, his knowing of this
new world is also the making of the new world
which he is coming to know.

R.G. Collingwood[1]

Dimensions of Encounter

The encounter with the reality of experience is manifold — a complex of
interaction. In the present encounter all that personal memory supplies is
potentially available from the past. Events in one's living, unique in themselves, nonetheless contain likenesses and associations by which they may
refer to other events. Were this not so, we should not be able, as we say, to
learn from experience. To learn from experience is both to reflect upon the
past and to project to the future. In artistic encounter we are confronted with
the need for form: without shape by which to give definition, experience
remains unembodied. The need for form involves us in an encounter with
the history of the culture of artistic form — traditions of disposing of the
symbols of art, traditions unique to a given society or shared among
societies. Within these traditions we find ways by which the formal characteristics of an art can lend themselves to the realization of individual experience. Art, we discover, is thus not an autistic exercise performed by the
esoteric and isolated personality, but is, in fact, part of the historic process of
a communal enterprise.

There is encounter with the *medium* of that art, whether visual, plastic,
kinetic, aural, or tactile — or combinations thereof. The medium employed
appeals directly to the senses and invokes an immediate response via the
senses. Dance, which includes gesture (and repertoires of gesture in the shape

of mime), appeals to us visually, but works through our sense of movement, an inward responsiveness silently gesticulating the outlines of meaning in space. Painting and sculpture similarly appeal most obviously to the visual sense; but not solely. We are drawn to examples of both through a perception of their tactile quality as well — the texture of paint on canvas, the tactile suggestiveness of materials and their surfaces used in a sculpture. This is so even if we are not allowed to touch the painting or the sculpture. This desire is often very strong in the latter case — to trace tactilely the sculpture's occupation of space in a sort of mimesis of form. (There are museums which now permit the blind and the partially-sighted to lay hands upon some sculptural exhibits so that they might be 'seen'). Language, the medium of literature, because of its capacity to render and to invoke imagistically impressions derived from all of the senses, including the kinaesthetic, likewise draws our sensuous appreciation and appraisal. Such potential of literary forms demands, however, a recognition of what language is and, in its fullness, what language can do.

It was W.H. Auden, I believe, who commented that a poet first falls in love with the language, and from this all else follows. It is what the love of language leads to which is important, not the infatuation itself. What the encounter with language makes possible is the making of things as expressions of experience, so that the realities they project vivify the experience of being alive. Such a love of language is a recognition of the fecund possibilities of the creative potential of language — what one can do with it. Whether, for the individual artist, the medium of language is or is not the first love, every creative encounter is an encounter with the symbolic system of that art — whether verbal, visual, plastic, aural, or kinetic. Verbal language, for the writer, is the chosen means by which to explore the reality of experience and so begin both to accommodate that reality and to come to terms with it. The making of a poem or a story is an active experiment with the language.

Language: a System of Systems, an Enterprise of Acts

The contemporary movement of structuralism and post-structuralism would make this experimentation with the *system* of language (sometimes dubbed 'a system of systems') the sole subject-matter of literature. In the making of a poem there is almost inevitably a certain moment, or a protracted period of time, in which the manipulation of the language appears to be the prime concern, the major preoccupation. What gave rise to this preoccupation, the motivation to occupy oneself on this occasion, may appear to become dissolved in the attention to language itself. That, however, is a far cry from the assertion of structuralists that that is *all* a poem is, an artefact of language made out of 'the tradition of disposing the possibilities of language to poetic ends', as David Lodge summarized the proposition.[2] To concede this fully would still not even begin to answer the question — usually, in such systematic contexts of analysis, not asked — *why* anyone would therefore wish to make one or more of these dispositions of language in the first place. Since there are plenty of poems about anyway, why make more of them?

The wry dismissiveness of E.M. Forster's assertion that he wrote novels in order to make money and to impress those persons he wished to impress, though amusing, simply will not do; and a reading of Forster's own *Aspects of the Novel* is eloquent testimony to the fact that it did not do for him either.[3] There is a point at which the determined reduction of a poem to a system of linguistic significations, by dispossessing the composer of her or his experience actually removes any *raison d'être* for the being of the piece in the first place. There must be *something* against which one tests the formation of the language as one assembles it, something to which the language is directed, other than the system of language itself. I have not yet met any poet who has agreed, when I have put the question, that she or he makes poems in order to make a construction of the systematic possibilities of the language. None has difficulties in recognizing that, in the making of the poem, the sustained endeavour, often over a very protracted period of time, is given to an attention to language — the active exploration of possibilities inherent within the symbolic system of signs which we call language. Clearly to compose anything one must have a system of language by which to compose; the system *makes possible* the articulation.

Without such a system the composer would make music without the symbolism of sound. John Cage's celebrated event of silence certainly did not compose music; it could not because silence is only one of the elements of music.[4] In fact, Cage's claim was, I believe, to have composed an event through which people would become acutely aware of the 'noise' of silence. Music of course, *employs* silence; it is a part of the language of music and absolutely vital to it. Clearly sounds do articulate themselves against silence — as do the sounds of speech; just as dance articulates its movement against stillness. These are other matters. But artists make art because they have something to say or because they wish to discover what it is they have to say. This is a good deal more than a modification of the language — it is the motivation *in the first place* to attempt to make the modification of the language. The purist forms of structuralist and post–structuralist critical ideology would seek to dispossess the artist of personal experience altogether. The matter has been admirably put by Denis Donoghue:

> Structuralists and Post-structuralists ... replace the author by language itself, which is then studied as an impersonal system, a system that doesn't need a person to work it. The idea is that language allows for a personal intervention in the moment of writing or speaking, but the person ceases with the enunciation... A critic who is interested in modern literature ... is supposed to find that the work of art is a mere function of a compromised language, corrupted because it has been used in the exercise of power and on behalf of an ideology ...[5]

In one sense the exercise of structuralism is an act of despair, for it does not acknowledge the possibility of renewal — of the making good of language, so 'to purify the dialect of the tribe', to borrow Eliot's expression from 'Little Gidding' (1942). If the *system* of language is diseased, all its offspring are distortions or misrepresentations of 'pure' meaning. The excesses of structuralist critiques and the methodologies they employ are attempts to immunize the reader-critic against the infection carried by the language she or he encounters. This is the very opposite of the liberal-humanist approach to literature which moved, not by cynicism, but by compassionate identification with 'the reek of the human', to import here Wordsworth's telling phrase. Structuralism distrusts the notion of 'meaning' itself, the intentionality of meaning, and the representation of experience through language — whilst it is manifestly the case that the whole endeavour of people's actual *use* of language is to make meaning. Such critics are right to point out that meaning is seldom a simple affair — but it is wrong to depersonalize language, since language does not exist outside of someone's use of it. Where else is language, but in what I write and speak and in what you say and write? Language is a human enterprise of *acts*. Denis Donoghue concludes:

> What do we gain by saying that T.S. Eliot's 'Gerontion' is a work of language, and that Eliot is merely its scribe? The point about a scribe is that someone else could do his work. To refuse to call the writing of 'Gerontion' a creative act performed with the collaboration of the English language is nonsense. The fact that the English language is a communal creation, the work of its speakers over many centuries, is not at all incompatible with the creative imagination we ascribe to Eliot in this instance. A linguistic system makes certain things possible, but makes nothing actual. Nothing could ever be done if it were left to a system to do it.[6]

In our teaching of literature we are not, I think, *primarily* engaged in language-study as a discipline of linguistics. We are very much involved with the system of language as it generates meaning within the context of utterance of the poem itself. To that end I think we need to approach language, the medium of creative utterance in literary forms, in a rather different fashion to that advocated by the structuralists. De Saussure's bequest of signs, signifiers and signifieds deals with language as a system, as a formal organization, but not with what is beyond the words; not what is *in* the words themselves, but what *by* the words is being articulated.[7]

Language and Symbolization

The place and function of language can be understood only in relation to the notion of symbolization. Experience itself, more precisely the experiencing of the passing moment, can not be handled directly. One is subject to a welter of impressions, a continuum of the unregistered and unordered flow of experience.[8] So much happens simultaneously or in a swift succession of impressions, all of our senses contributing to the state of *now*. What constitutes our apprehension of any moment is, in fact, a selection from all that we are experiencing, and a concentration upon those particular evidences of the senses. All of the rest which, in the moment itself, 'passes us by' may not, however, be irretrievably lost. Indeed, there are occasions when only after the event do we become aware of the event, details of which the recollecting agency of memory can bring to mind. Since immediate sense-impression has gone with the fleeting moment, it can pass unmediated by cognition. If the impression of experience is to be reflected upon, examined, and acted upon retrospectively, there must be some intermediate means for its retrieval. That means of 'calling to mind' the past is provided through the transformation of experience into symbols. Between the experiential moment and the recall of the history of that moment stands the symbol:

> The material furnished by the senses is constantly wrought into *symbols*, which are our elementary ideas. Some of these ideas can be combined and manipulated in the manner we call 'reasoning'. Others do not lend themselves to this use, but are naturally telescoped into dreams, or vapor off in conscious fantasy; and a vast number of them build the most typical edifice of the human mind — religion.[9]

Sensory experience is recalled, in part, through various sensory images. But these are residual impressions only of past experience. They provide some of the raw data, as it were, with which to begin the building of elementary ideas. The difference, in this setting, between image and symbol resides in the suggestive power of the latter to *transform* experience rather than simply to furnish a memorized *replication* of experience. Susanne Langer's philosophy of symbolic transformation, following on the work of Ernst Cassirer, goes on from the passage quoted above to point out that it is the symbol-making ability of the human brain which makes possible a wide variety of different symbolic activities. Different kinds of symbolization make possible different modes of behaviour: but what these share in common is the 'expression of ideas':

> The fact that the human brain is constantly carrying on a process of symbolic transformation of the experiential data that comes to it causes it to be a veritable fountain of more or less spontaneous ideas. As all registered experience tends to terminate in action, it is only natural that a typically human function should require a typically human form of overt activity; and that is just what we find in *the sheer expression of ideas*. This is the activity of which beasts appear to have no need. And it accounts for just those traits in man which he does not hold in common with the other animals — ritual, art, laughter, weeping, speech, superstition, and scientific genius.[10]

Symbolic expression is a manifest of the ideas, in whatever rudimentary form, held by or within the presented symbols. An image represents a segment of experience, but a symbol already begins to form an idea of that from which it derives or that to which it might refer. Symbols are *worked experience*, human intelligence effecting a transformation to make them ideational; they relate to conception, or, in Susanne Langer's own words, symbolization 'is the starting-point of all intellection...' Here, again, is a powerful argument for the symbolic ordering of experience which the arts supply. Art, employing (even though not exclusively) sensuous experience can not be 'senseless', for the representation of that experience already begins to move into a form whose symbolization itself is made of the very stuff from which ideas are compounded. Art is creative intelligence.

The existence of symbols makes possible their combination, so that new symbolic connections and contiguities can be formed, networks of symbolic constructions fashioned, patterns made. Symbolization includes not only a vocabulary of symbols, but a grammar also. There is a language. Improvisation of the system produces new symbolic versions of the language.

Symbolization is a transformation of experience; it is the process by which experience can be expressed. More than that, however, the symbolic system makes possible a *representation* of experience, makes it available to second and subsequent awareness. It becomes an integral part of the symbol-making resource, a means by which one can *act symbolically* even in the absence of actual, immediate and direct, experience. Every work of art, in whatever medium, is such a symbolic act.

Of the symbolic modes by which we express experience it is language itself which has become the most elaborated, the most flexive, and the one most readily available to us. Highly developed, it enables us to make abstractions — to use the symbolic system itself to explore the symbolization (as, in a simple case, where we try to 'define' what it is we have already said). Language is also the most common of symbolic modes, in the sense that it is the symbolic process to which most of us have recourse on most occasions. Through language we can respond in a moment (at times a disadvantage). We have an immediacy of access to it, and turn to speech, more or less fluently, to express ourselves. The universality of the phenomenon of speech and its sheer abundance can conceal its symbolization, the real nature of what seems commonplace. For language has become the principal means by which we categorize experience — the means by which we make representation, and thus the realities we make of experience.

Symbolic Transformation

The remarkable life, and the equally remarkable testimony, of Helen Keller should remind us of the transforming effects and consequences which the symbolization of language makes possible. Having lost both sight and hearing at a very early stage of infancy, she learned, from her teacher Miss Sullivan, to spell on her fingers the letters of the word for 'doll' — though at the time, as she expressed it, 'I did not know that I was spelling a word or even that words existed; I was simply making my fingers go in monkey-like imitation.'[11] Similarly, she learned to spell 'in this uncomprehending way' a great many other words. But the symbolic connection of *word* (a concept she had not developed) and the sense-impressions of an *object* had not been established. That transfiguration of her world of experience is recorded in the following passage of her *Autobiography* — a passage well-known, its very familiarity sometimes obscuring the profound significance of what Helen Keller discovered. On the day of her revelation her teacher had tried again to make symbolic connections through spelling on her fingers:

> One day, while I was playing with my new doll, Miss Sullivan put my big rag doll into my lap also, spelled 'd-o-l-l' and tried to make me understand that 'd-o-l-l' applied to both. Earlier in the day we had a tussle over the words 'm-u-g' and 'w-a-t-e-r'. Miss Sullivan had tried to impress it upon me that 'm-u-g' is *mug* and that 'w-a-t-e-r' is *water*, but I persisted in confounding the two.[12]

The nature of the symbolization of words eluded her. Then Miss Sullivan brought the child's hat to her. Through a 'wordless sensation' the child knew she was going out into the warm sunshine:

> We walked down the path to the well-house, attracted by the fragrance of the honeysuckle with which it was covered. Some one was drawing water and my teacher placed my hand under the spout. As the cool stream gushed over one hand she spelled into the other the word *water*, first slowly, then rapidly. I stood still, my whole attention fixed upon the motions of her fingers. Suddenly I felt a misty consciousness of something forgotten — a thrill of returning thought; and somehow the mystery of language was revealed to me. I knew then that 'w-a-t-e-r' meant the wonderful cool something that was playing over my hand. That living word awakened my soul, gave it light, hope, joy, set it free! There were barriers still, it is true, but barriers that could in time be swept away.
>   I left the well-house eager to learn. Everything had a name, and each name gave birth to a new thought. As we returned to the house every object which I touched seemed to quiver with life. That was because I saw everything with the strange, new sight that had come to me.[13]

'Everything had a name, and each name gave birth to a new thought.' The recognition of the relationship of word to the idea of object transformed Helen Keller's life. The symbolizing system of language made 'thinking' possible, and thus made possible a conceiving of the world and thus the nature of the ways in which she would continue to experience her existence.

For there to be thought there must be something to think *with*, since one can not think with the objects, events and circumstances of the world itself. With characteristic percipience Coleridge pre-dated again much of the contemporary theorizing concerned with establishing the essential activity of thinking. In a letter to William Godwin he laid out a prospectus for reflection:

> ... Is *thinking* impossible without arbitrary signs? & how far is the word 'arbitrary' a misnomer? Are not words, &c. parts & germinations of the Plant? And what is the Law of their Growth? — In something of this order I would endeavour to destroy the old antithesis of *Words & Things* elevating, as it were, words into Things, and living Things too.[14]

For Coleridge language was not simply an instrument of thinking but was the source of thought; it did not merely enable thinking to proceed, it initiated thinking. Language already contained thought — a position close to Langer's expression of the matter. In a letter written much later than that addressed to Godwin, Coleridge had refined his view. In the following excerpt from a letter to James Gillman he proposed this intimacy between thought and language:

> It is the fundamental mistake of grammarians and writers on the philosophy of language to suppose that words and their syntaxis are the immediate representatives of *things*, or that they correspond to *things*. Words correspond to thoughts, and the legitimate order and connection of words to the *laws* of thinking and to the acts and affections of the thinker's mind.[15]

In part Coleridge's speculative proposals were a reaction against the traditional view of language and thought which he had inherited. In this explanation thought and language were conceived as separate entities. It was believed that 'thought' first occurred to the mind, and its expression was then made after a conscious search for those words which would most appropriately convey the 'meaning' of the thought. Thought thereby had an independent existence which preceded any expression of itself. It followed, too, that there could be an infinite number of expressions of the same thought. This, precisely, is what Alexander Pope summarized in the following lines:

> *True Wit* is *Nature* to Advantage drest,
> What oft was *Thought*, but ne'er so well *Exprest*,
> *Something*, whose Truth convinc'd at Sight we find,
> That gives us back the Image of our Mind —
>
> (From: *An Essay on Criticism*, 1711, I, 297–300)[16]

It was Wit, as originality (and brevity) of expression, whether amusing or not, which was the valued quality of thought; and the heroic couplet lent itself admirably to the Augustans' search for compression and epigrammatic tautness. The concentration upon Wit, a quality of thought, also explains those reputations made, and eagerly sought, as conversationalists. But throughout, there was no perception of the essential bonding of language and the expression of thought.

Representation and Realization

Today linguists, psychologists, and others would generally agree that there are various ways in which representations of individual reality are possible, via their different schema.[17] Many would agree that there are different ways of operating upon, or processing experience; some would accept that these different forms of human behaviour might all be referred to as 'thinking' — purposive, intelligent behaviour which can solve problems and resolve difficulties through direct action. Following the work of Vygotsky,[18] it is possible to conceive of a 'post-language' symbolization operating in place of internalized speech in mature thinking — that is, a mode of thinking, derived from language, which no longer employs the formal characteristics of language. The 'language' which conducts this thinking becomes abbreviated, and the organization of its 'meaning-units' diverges from the conventions of syntax. A 'meaning-unit', as Vygotsky expressed it, is 'a word so saturated with sense that many words would be required to explain it in external speech'.[19] Such post-language symbols are hypothesised as a kind of after-effect of language, of the inner speech through which we first learn to conduct those monologues of language which we call thinking.

Vygotsky's use of the term 'sense' distinguishes the significance of a word from that ordinarily assigned to it in dictionary or explicit meaning. This seems to me true of conventional words as well as of supposed post-language symbols. By 'sense', Vygotsky refers us to all of the psychological events aroused in our consciousness by the use of the word. Such psychological events may be triggered in any region of consciousness; thus we may not be knowingly aware of the response, but it may well help to explain how we attach feeling to words and word-combinations. They mean more to us than we can say.

In one way what Vygotsky is pointing to is an extension of the nominative function of language. It is one of the first uses of language developed by the child, and it makes possible, as the history of Helen Keller so graphically illustrates, the management of the world of experience. Words, then combinations of words, provide symbolic representations of our experience of the actualities of object, event, and process. The naming itself begins to construe a representation of reality. Once named, the nature of what we had taken to be the reality may also change. Contrarily, experience which is *not* named, though a fact of living experience, can remain remote from our apprehension of it. Peter McKellar,[20] for example, from his practice as a psychologist, recounted the story of a woman troubled by a repeated experience. After listening to her accounts McKellar named her experiences as instances of *déjà vu*. The naming in itself gave relief to the woman and provided a reassurance. Immediately (even though the naming itself is not an explanation) the woman became less troubled. For the act of naming *transformed the nature of the reality of experience* from one which she had perceived as private to one which she could now see as shared and social. It was not she alone who had such experiences, and the word liberated her from her insularity. Symbolically transformed, the incomprehensibility and strangeness of her experience could then be confronted, examined, and come to terms with. The subjective experience (to return to an earlier theme) achieved an objective, social reality. The transforming agent, relating and uniting the two, existed in the middle-state of language. This, precisely, is what happens with each endeavour to make literary writings — though the nature of experience being attended to is far more extensive than that which can be accommodated in a simple act of 'naming' in a word or two. Frequently the 'naming' of experience requires elaborate devices of language, the constructions of whole poems, novels, and other forms of literature.

The principle of what happened, in the example of *déjà vu* cited above, is repeated daily on innumerable occasions. In 'talking things over' with a confidant(e) — whether a friend in the home, the pub or office; the therapist in a study; the priest in the confessional — we try to 'find the words' which, in the first place, give *us* a proper sense of whatever experience it is we are attempting to express. Again and again one hears, as the listener, 'No, what I mean is ...'; a qualifying, amending, and substitution of one formulation of the language for another, each successive attempt aiming to get closer and closer to the particular character of experience so that it satisfies the speaker. In the most seemingly-casual of encounters one is witnessing language being used creatively to express a realization of self, an acknowledgment of experience, *driven by a need to make sense*. It is a drive to make sense for oneself; it is not always an essential requirement of the speaker that the other person shall understand as well. Often it is so, but not on every occasion, as this overheard remark conveys: 'Well, I haven't a clue what she was trying to say, but she seemed a lot brighter when she went...' The tenor of this comment I am sure can be confirmed by every reader of this book; it is a commonplace of our social lives. It seems that the mere presence of another person can be the inducement we require to speak out, to find a form of words which locates and represents our thoughts. In some way the attempt to communicate our experience makes us use words in a manner different from that in which we have revolved the matter in the seclusion of our own heads. It makes us take into account matters for which we had not perhaps accounted in that private cerebration. Utterance is an act of 'outering' experience. When the language has been so manifested, we are free to engage with the possibilities of language itself as a surrogate representative of experience. Once uttered the language is, so to speak, 'out there' — an objective representation of subjective experience; we can then relate to *it*, the language. We can 'see if it says what we think we mean', and continue to refine and amend and qualify the language itself until we shape a satisfying expression to which we can relate. For language itself contains meanings within meanings. We can operate upon the symbolic transformation, which is the language, instead of trying to handle experience directly. Once symbolically transformed we are freed to explore further and so to refine more closely the representation we have made to the point where it feels right; the representation becomes valid as an authentic expression of consciousness.

Expression and Experience

Here is a more complex illustration of the symbolization of language to express experience. Paul, as I shall call him, was fourteen and like many of his contemporaries he was biding his time before leaving school to get a job. He was a generally quiet pupil who never made himself particularly noticeable in the classroom. He was not indifferent to work, indeed at times he was capable of quite sustained concentration, but he never had much to say for himself. He would respond, if prompted, but would not volunteer.

Paul had never before written a poem, had never attempted to. Following a session in which, through various activities I introduced to the class the idea of composing their own poems, I found the following among the batch of writings submitted to me. It was neatly written, but unsigned.

Run Murderer

The fear in his heart grew,
The sorrow for himself showed in his eyes.
The body was still warm.
So he ran, ran, ran.

He still ran as they chased him,
He began to hate the mob.
Yet the body was still warm.
So he ran, ran, ran.

The fear in his heart grew,
The sorrow for himself showed in his eyes.
The body was still warm.
So he ran, ran, ran.

He still ran as they caught him,
He still ran as they killed him.
Yet the body was now cold.
So he ran.

My first response to the poem was to see it either as a part of a 'dream-sequence' or as an episode derived from a 'thriller' film. Several days passed and the poem slipped from my mind. Finally, however, Paul came to see me at the end of one lesson, and not until then did I discover the identity of the author of the piece. Paul, however, wanted to talk to me, not about the poem, but about himself. He had done something which he later knew to be very wrong. He imagined, not without cause, that if he were discovered he would land himself in trouble. Consequently he had been 'running away' both from what he had done and from what might happen to him if he were found out. Yet he had not been able to out-distance his sense of guilt in the matter, even though his 'crime' was some time ago and 'the body was now cold'. What is striking in this example, I believe, is the fact that here *artistic shaping preceded the speaking out of experience.* In listening to Paul it soon became very clear that his grasp of his own circumstances owed much to the first articulation in the form of the poem; a precise illustration, we might say, of 'parable art'. I think it is worth passing comment, too, that the expression of this disturbance demanded a form through which it might achieve substance; in this case, a fairly regular form, made tighter by the refrain and the insistent rhythms. Based on a conventional quatrain arrangement, though with some variation both of line length and rhythms among the stanzas, the poem shows how the formal properties of a traditional pattern can be used, not as a template, but as a screen through which to see a possible organization. It is often the case that where there is great personal disturbance there is great need for the discipline of strict form.[21] Chaotic experience, if it is to be represented at all, though contrary to what we may first logically propose, can seldom, if ever, be projected as artistic chaos. Without the organizing principle of form there can be no perception of the nature of the chaos. For art moves towards *meaning*, and this is what distinguishes it immediately from mere self-expression. To express myself I may heave a brick through a window, or, as did the boys in Edward Bond's play *Saved* (1965), senselessly stone a baby to death. Self-expression need not be wholesome; it can be negative and destructive also. Or, as with the spurious 'happening' art of the 1960s, to express myself I may organize an event; then I shall smash up a piano and pass the bits through a musical triangle hanging from a butcher's hook, or I shall attempt to spit orange pips through a wedding ring at a distance of ten paces whilst spinning a hula-hoop around my waist. There are many ways in which I might express myself. Self-expression may be a sign or act of the symptoms of my state or condition, and such acts may well have a cathartic effect upon me, but they do not in themselves move me any closer either to a delineation or understanding of the reality of my experience. Self-expression can take a form known by some of the French existentialists as *l'acte gratuite*. But the movement of self into the expression of an art-form, because it is a search for meaning, is not gratuitous; it is a movement towards health, to a sense of self in relation to the whole world of experience — a resolution and a balance. That is the drive in art-making whether or not the individual artist achieves that harmony. The popular equation between artists and madness is here the wrong way round. It is not the art which makes them mad, but the art through which they are striving to save themselves. (Though I am not at all convinced that there are proportionately more 'mad' artists than there are 'mad' doctors, driving instructors, computer programmers, or politicians. Perhaps other professions of madness simply do not come to our notice?)

I do not wish to be understood to be arguing that art arises exclusively from the psychopathology of the artist, and that the making of art is psychotherapy. On occasion, and in an individual instance, either or both of these dimensions of personality may be true. I certainly would not attempt to detract from the various 'art as therapy' movements which have proved to have so much of advantage to offer to individual persons — their art-makings aiding both diagnosis and 'treatment'. Certainly I am sure that many teachers, of whichever art discipline, occasionally have encountered pupils who, like Paul, have made art-forms which enabled them to face their own experience. But what we make in art is not simply an esoteric 'expression' of a private condition. If it were so, there would be no means by which any person would be able to enter the artwork of any other person without having first the identical autobiographical record of experience. And art is clearly communal; it enters a culture. There it may be encountered by others because it 'impersonalizes' (it does not *de*personalize) experience by its representativeness, because the symbols it employs are not the exclusive possession of the artist. Authentic art is thereby also a *sharing* — a predisposition which may go deep into our social beings. In literature we employ a medium, language itself, which is social; it belongs to the society and to each individual.

Language and Meaning: Creative Improvisation

Returning to Paul's poem we can see that the poem acts as a metaphor. It is a moral fable. Within it the inarticulate meaning of experience has found a voice, and the subjectivity of self is extended into the object of the poem. Language and form have created a setting which locates Paul's private experience at a remove. Because language contains the possibilities of meanings within meanings, words can refer outside their immediate context and be 'seen' within other frameworks of meaning. The poem could 'stand for' a class of experiences of which Paul's was one in particular. The poem may identify something of the feelings of guilt and of being pursued by one's guilt across a wide variety of individual, and different 'crimes'. The symbolization of language makes possible, at this remove, the location of experience. In Paul's case the impetus towards meaning was personal, the subject (Paul) achieving an articulation in the object (poem). Some literature may proceed from a larger degree of objectivity — the projected contents of the work arising not from actual and personal experience, but from others' real or imagined events. The engagement with the making will nonetheless be personal, a subjective realization of the possibilities of the objectively-proposed. Though clearly a more elaborated procedure, essentially this is typically what some novelists may do; there are also many examples of poetry following the same procedure. The novelist puts characters (figmented from experience) into settings where things may happen, where characters may encounter each other, and the author can 'see what happens'. Such a procedure cannot be equated solely, and only in a very simplistic way, with 'self-expression'. It is an experiment with meaning. The author, in advance of the final composition, may have a good idea what will happen in order to demonstrate a selected theme, or almost no idea at all. D.H. Lawrence expressed the latter view:

> The novels and poems come quite unwatched out of one's pen. And then the absolute need one has for some sort of satisfactory attitude towards oneself and things in general makes one try to abstract some definite conclusions from one's experience as a writer and a man.[22]

Lawrence here alludes to two modes of thinking, the intuitive circumscription of implied meaning (through the creative acts of making novels and poems), and the deductive reasoning out, the explication, of that meaning. Employing differing terminology and descriptions, a distinction between two modes of thinking has been maintained by psychologists as diverse as Pavlov, Freud, Jung, and Spearman — and has been reinforced by a good deal of research in neuropsychology.[23] What Lawrence is acknowledging, in fact, is the way in which a complex of unformulated experience may be revealed by subjecting that experience in its wholeness to the symbolization of language. Then it may be worked over, as it were, through analysis and the other rational discriminatory processes of thinking. Of course, the two typified forms of thinking are not mutually exclusive, nor are they always kept separate in any artistic endeavour; all artists are likely at some point to engage in directed, analytical thinking-through of the work-in-hand so as to make it more precisely what, as it emerges, it appears to be. In Lawrence's case the immediacy of the presentation of experience is frequently qualified instantly with what he termed 'pollyanalytics' — 'inferences made afterwards from the experience'.[24]

Writers work with a variable mix of intuition and deliberateness; what they produce in a work results in measure from their symbolization of what Michael Polanyi recognized as 'tacit knowledge',[25] a knowledge which can be 'known' or identified only when it has achieved some form of utterance, an 'outering' of its inherent nature in language or some other symbolic representation. The testimony of Lawrence is exactly paralleled in a remark ascribed to E.M. Forster: 'How can I know what I think till I see what I write?' There is a thinking which is in the *doing*, in the making of poem or novel, which makes manifest (though not necessarily explicit) what the writer 'knows' in the context in which the writing is proceeding. In this sense there is an intimate relationship between thinking and the act of speech itself.

Since I first came across the following remark cited by the Danish philologist, Otto Jesperson, from a contemporary novel of the time, I have always been struck by its resonant implications. In Housman's *John of Jingalo* a young girl says:

> *I talk so as to find out what I think. Don't you? Some things one can't judge of til one hears them spoken.*[26]

I believe the truth of this passing comment in fact refers us to the very stream of consciousness itself from which springs, not only speech, but the variety of art-forms we make *in* language *with* language. The contemporaneity of speech and thought, thinking virtually simultaneous with the act of speaking, confirms the centrality of talk to the educative process of the child — a fact which sociolinguists have emphasized. That children and older students alike should be encouraged 'to speak their minds', in order to discover what it is they are thinking, is clearly of vital importance across the whole curriculum. In the context of literature-teaching the speaking of minds has especial significance. There are opportunities here for students to engage, through what Lawrence called 'art-speech', with works of literature, to discover about themselves in relation to the work. There is preparatory talk, prior to the making of their own literary writings, which enables them both to identify and to focus upon the essential experiences of which the writing will be compounded. There is exchange of talk, the sharing of experience, perceptions, views. There is also collaborative talk, students mutually engaged and directed to the realization of a joint enterprise. There is the rehearsal and improvisation of the speech of poetry and dialogue by which they can come to a realization of the sound-values of speech itself and the ways in which these potently contribute to the delineation of meaning and significance — the shape of utterance through its aural qualities. The discipline of writing, the students' own created forms and the expressive criticism of other works, adds another dimension to the speaking of minds. In writing they can begin to explore modes of utterance which break free of the tyranny of sequentiality — writing which, though line-by-line, compounds meaning in a molecular fashion with internal self-referencing. Through talk and writing our students can experiment with alternative ways of using language to generate meaning: a gestalt of meaning which is the poem or the story, not the discursive track of language which is their dominant experience of language outside of literary forms.

Making Sense: Making Meaning

We are, as Polanyi so clearly demonstrated, aware of so much more than we 'know', can positively identify, or can state explicitly. This is the 'tacit dimension' in which we live, a dimension derived from all that we have ever been, the totality of experience. It is the 'sense' we have made of being, but it is unformulated. It is inarticulate. Even in the nominative function of language there are 'subsidiary' processes which have gone into the word to denote experience. Among Polanyi's examples is the following, which I have selected because it also throws some light upon other symbolizing operations, such as that of painting, and the case of Cézanne to which I referred in an earlier section:

> Our conception of a tree, for example, is formed ... by the tacit integration of countless experiences of different trees and pictures and reports of still others, deciduous and evergreen, straight and crooked, bare and leafy. All these encounters are included in forming the conception of a tree, which is what we mean by the word 'tree'.[27]

Polanyi's observation accords well with Vygotsky's notion of the 'sense' of a word and its 'meaning'. It is in this distinction that we can locate the difficulties which many pupils, and older students, too, have (especially, but not exclusively) with poetry — the 'reading' of poetry. They approach the task with a certain view of what language is, of what words are. They tend, in the main, to see words as analogues of things, or of discrete meanings such as a dictionary will identify for them. They do not see that such a view makes the artist in words a servant to the language, rather than its master. They do not appreciate that words are possessed by the individual, and that therefore their sense far exceeds their meaning — as, again, Coleridge (in his *Biographia Literaria*, 1817) alerted us to before either Polanyi or Vygotsky made their formulations:

> Be it observed ... that I include in the meaning of a word not only its correspondent word alone, but likewise all the associations which it recalls. For language is framed to convey not the object alone, but likewise the character, mood and intentions of the person who is representing it.[28]

If this were not so we would not be able to make language a personal construction of meaning. It is this fact of language which structuralist critics in their 'writerly' readings of literary works have stressed in their search for what they refer to as the author's 'ideologies', though at times what they discover is a reflection of their own ideologies from which predisposition they proceeded in their search. It is the cycle of self-fulfilling prophecies which the committed Marxist or feminist critic (or critic wishing to espouse any other ideology) must prove in her or his writings, which then 'cover' (in Barthes's term)[29] the original text. Though we can leave aside the gratuitous and the distorting examples to which such procedures may lead, the central realization of structuralism — the extensive nature of signification — must be acknowledged. Whether explicitly stated or, as is most often the case, sublimated in and implicit to the text, the meaning of an author's work engages us in contextual discrimination through a recognition of the multiple nature of sense which emerges from a complex of the meanings of words. What we must retain, however, is the human dimension of meaning; meaning not simply as a product of the arrangement of the linguistic system, but as a product of the maker — an exercise of consciousness in its attempt to make awareness.

There are ideologies of author or reader which may be individual. These are a personal cast of personality. There are others which more clearly belong to a social, usually implicit, set of values. In addition, there can be scholarly implications in our critical encounter with a text. There is the fact of language change — the shift of meanings attached to a word as the use of the word changes historically. There is the contrary fact that, though the word has not changed, the values attaching to the word from one age to another have undergone radical alteration. We would not proceed very far, and certainly with little understanding, if we did not comprehend what the contemporary notion of 'kingship' implies when we read Shakespeare's histories. Thus the possible range of sense with which a word can be saturated may be far more extensive even than that indicated by Coleridge.

Literary writing at some point confronts the prescription of meaning as derived from analogue to object or dictionary definition. For the meaning of the word derives its sense from the context of its location — its sense as it is involved in the implicatory system of meanings which is the whole poem (or other work). There are many ways in which teachers attempt to bring this awareness to their students, but the most assured way of all is through the students' own engagement with their personal literary writings. This is the most certain way of enabling them *to see for themselves* how meanings, and the complex of sense which they generate, are fashioned out of their interaction with language. By investigating, within the literary context, what language can do, they will more assuredly recognize the same or related effects in those literary forms of mature writers which they will encounter. In the case of a poem, for example, students may be helped to perceive that the sense of a poem derives from its network of meanings, and that such a network is not linear and sequential (such as in a telephone directory), but is molecular. Any word may relate to any other words within the space of the poem — not just to those words with which it is in sequential contiguity.

The literary writer encounters language in its fullness in the shaping of those representations by which symbolic transformations of experience, actual or imagined, may be effected. What one brings *to* the encounter substantially affects the form within which one attempts the realization of experience. The encounter is not singular, with the system of language only. It is a reciprocal engagement; of experience with language, and of language with experience. Language can change the nature of experience; experience can force changes in language. But experience cannot be disassociated from language, for language would then become an exclusively abstract system. In the literary encounter with language the exploring word symbolizes its space between the actuality of experience and the system of language from which it derives. Through language we again explore the meanings of that created territory.

Notes and References

1 Collingwood, R.G. (1975) *The Principles of Art*, Oxford, Oxford University Press, p. 291.
2 Lodge, D. (1981) *Working With Structuralism*, London, Routledge and Kegan Paul, p. 5.
3 Forster, E.M. (1974) *Aspects of the Novel and Related Writings*, London, Edward Arnold.
4 Cage, J. (1966) *Silence*, Cambridge, MA and London, MIT Press.
5 Donoghue, D. (1989) 'The Domestication of Outrage', in Abbs, P. (Ed.), *The Symbolic Order*, London, Falmer Press, pp. 110–111.
6 *Ibid.*, p. 111. Though not so directed in Donoghue's own text, this passage may be read most profitably against Roland Barthes's essay 'The Death of the Author' in Barthes, R. (1977) *Image — Music — Text*, trans. Heath, S., London, Fontana.
7 de Saussure, F. (1983) *Course in General Linguistics*, London, Duckworth.
8 Based on the work of Weltner, K. (1973) *The Measurement of Verbal Information in Psychology and Education*, trans. Crook, B.M., Berlin, Heidelberg and New York, Springer-Verlag, E.L. Epstein offers the following summary of the ceaseless flow of sensory information:

> A million bits of information enter the eye every second; the skin, the nasal passages, the mouth, the musculature, the semi-circular canals of the ear, all of these constantly experience an unremitting barrage of signals. Even silence is not silent; the collision of molecules of air can occasionally be heard as a shrill hiss. Every time your nerves 'change', you have received 'information'... We ignore vast amounts of information. We notice, or 'apperceive', about ten to twenty bits of information per second out of thousands of millions. A concert pianist, working at top capacity, can notice up to twenty-two bits of visual information per second. However even this reduced flow is not retained; most people can only retain in their long-term memory the equivalent of two to six bits per second. This adds up to an enormous number of recollections of aural stimuli in a lifetime. (Epstein, E.L. (1978) *Language and Style*, London, Methuen, p. 4)

What is true of the retention of aural experience is true too of experience derived from the other senses. The sheer vastness of such living experience adds further weight to Polanyi's assertion of the 'tacit dimension' of knowing. (See Select Bibliography)

9 Langer, S.K. (1960) *Philosophy in a New Key*, 3rd. edn., Cambridge, MA, Harvard University Press, p. 42.
10 *Ibid.*, p. 43.
11 Keller, H. (1958) *The Story of My Life*, London, Hodder and Stoughton, p. 25.
12 *Ibid.*, p. 26.
13 *Ibid.*
14 In Griggs, E.L. (Ed.) (1956–59) *The Collected Letters of Samuel Taylor Coleridge*, Oxford, Oxford University Press, I, pp. 625–6.
15 *Op. cit.*, VI, p. 126.
16 In Butt, J. (Ed.) (1968) *The Poems of Alexander Pope*, corrected edn., London, Methuen, p. 153.
17 One of the most influential of such formulations has been that of Jerome S. Bruner's classification of *enactive, iconic*, and *symbolic* systems of representation (in Bruner, J.S. (1967) *Towards a Theory of Instruction*, Harvard, Belknap Press).
18 Vygotsky, L.S. (1962) *Thought and Language*, trans. Haufman, E. and Vakar, G., Cambridge, MA, MIT Press.
19 Vygotsky, *ibid.*, p. 148.
20 McKellar, P. (1957) *Imagination and Thinking*, London, Cohen and West, p. 54.
21 John Pudney, in the Notes to a sequence of sonnets in his *Collected Poems* (1957, London, Putnam), tells of entering Paris, when the city was 'still noisy', with the French Forces of the Liberation in 1944:

> Pablo Picasso was painting a conventional picture of a pot of flowers when I entered his studio... He said, with a shrug, that the best thing one could do was to immerse oneself in a conventional form of art, adding that, as a writer, I should be doing sonnets. In indifferent French, I explained that I was.

22 Foreword to (1961) *Fantasia of the Unconscious*, London, Heinemann, p. 9.
23 In 1969 Dr. Joseph E. Bogen published an extensive review (with close to 400 references) of the evidences derived from neuro-surgery and neurological psychology. He concluded that in addition to the logical-reasoning of Propositional thinking, there was (what he called) Appositional thinking, to distinguish between the functions typically lateralized between the two hemispheres of the brain. Creativity, whether in the arts or the sciences, he concluded, required 'the cultivation and collaboration of the appositional mind'. ('The Other Side of the Brain', (1969) *Bulletin of the Los Angeles Neurological Societies*, 34).
24 *Fantasia of the Unconscious, op. cit.*, p. 9.
25 Polanyi's conception and elaboration of tacit knowledge, first identified in *Personal Knowledge* (1958) can be further traced through *The Tacit Dimension* (1958) and *Knowing and Being* (1969) — all London, Routledge and Kegan Paul.
26 Housman, L. *John of Jingalo*, London, Chapman and Hall, 1912, cited by Jesperson, O. (1922) *Language: its Nature, Development and Origin*, London, Allen and Unwin, p. 252. Jesperson in fact quotes the young girl's remark as an example of 'the volubility of women' — a comment which misses entirely the construction I have placed upon it; such talk is a condition of speech, not an exclusive possession of one sex.
27 Michael Polanyi, *Knowing and Being*, p. 191. In pursuit of the validity of this comment one could trace the progress of Cézanne's trees, from their more individualistic and representationally-detailed forms through to the *Sous-Bois* of 1895 and the *Landscape Near Aix* of a few years later. In the attempt to get closer

to the underlying form (conception) of 'tree' both of these two paintings become more abstract and, though separated in time and place, have a remarkable similarity each to the other.

28 Watson, G. (Ed.) (1965) *Biographia Literaria*, corrected edn., London, Dent, p. 263.
29 Barthes, R. (1972) 'What is Criticism?' in *Critical Essays*, trans. Howard, R., Evanston, Northwestern University Press, p. 259.

Part II

Feeling, Making, and Coming to Know Personally

The primacy of human feeling operates as an integer of virtually the whole of human behaviour. In art-making feeling persists as a latent recognition of the value of experience, and the impulse to create may start in the need to explore and to come to terms with that tacit awareness. Feeling provides information about the self — a reflexive awareness of how experience affects us. The exploration of feeling-states can promote the conception of the literary writing, and provide a reference against which the emerging form of the work can be tested. For feeling can generate perceptions by which one comes to know personally both one's own world and, through a subjective extension of self, the worlds of others. When embodied in symbolic form, feeling has cognitive value; there, in the completed art-form, experience may be recognized, its character now available to scrutiny through the articulation of the literary work. The engagement of feeling becomes one of the prime objectives in the encouragement of students' own literary writings: and provides, through this making, important means of access to the literary experience of other texts.

Chapter 5

Patterns of Sentience

> I am always puzzled to know
> what I feel or how I feel.
>
> D.H. Lawrence[1]

Feeling and Personality

In the encounter with experience we engage the primacy of our feeling. We speak of our feelings, to denote what we *are feeling*. It is an important distinction; for what we feel is an active operation of consciousness. Only after the event, subsequent to our formulation, through some form of symbolic projection of what was being felt, can we then properly speak of *a* feeling. What we were feeling is now embodied, the processes of our experience now given articulation and shape. In the various forms of art that feeling finds distinctive and representative expression, a projection with which we can interact. The attempt to make some kind of representation of feeling induces an active exploration of its particular constitution, its realization. We may then *re-cognize* the character of our feeling on that occasion as experiencing individuals.

However we may seek to define feeling, we are confronted always with something elusive, almost fugitive, as Lawrence acknowledged. For as soon as we start to attend to our feeling, we have changed the nature of the feeling itself. If we think about our feeling, we have instantly begun to endow the experience with other qualities; we have begun to give feeling cognitive dimensions. Thus, we have to admit to the tentativeness of feeling. It is subjective, in the strict sense that it belongs to the subject, the individual who is feeling. In this regard, alone, resides much of the cause for those suspicious glances cast towards the arts and literature by those who would assert that reason and rationality are the highest of our evolutionary achievements. The propositional thought of the intellect seems to provide us with knowledge which is more definite, which has an externality to it; because it is 'out there' it may be examined, scrutinized, debated, agreed, rejected, amended. This is the knowledge whose mode of thinking and learning occupies the greatest amount of time in our educational curriculum, the timetable of 'subjects' through which we amass (or fail to) knowledge of things outside ourselves. In an age of quantification and operationalism, such knowledge is highly prized, and often rewarded highly; it is certainly promoted and encouraged by those who think of themselves as living in 'the real world'. The trouble is that such a world, on its own, may prove disappointing and breed disenchantment.

The record of John Stuart Mill's education is well known. It remains nonetheless a powerful exemplum. Indoctrinated at an early age into uniquely intellectual modes of thinking and of knowledge, there developed for him over many years a sense of unfulfilled development which, in maturity, he was able to perceive for himself. In his search for a more thorough integration of personality he came to the poems of William Wordsworth. What made those poems a medicine for his state of mind, he wrote:

> ... was that they expressed, not mere outward beauty, but states of feeling and of thought coloured by feeling, under the excitement of beauty. They seemed to be the very culture of the feelings I was in quest of.[2]

If education fails to take account of the need to recognize the primacy of human feeling — both to stimulate us to an awareness of our feeling and to stimulate us to new awareness *through* feeling — then the effect upon the individual can lead only to a diminution of what David Holbrook so appropriately called 'powers of being'.[3]

If the arteries of feeling harden, the development of personality is stunted. There may result a dehumanization, taking many forms. The lack of feeling is a pathological condition. The suppression of feeling can, in just one of its manifestations, induce what Ian D. Suttie decades ago presciently described as 'The Taboo on Tenderness',[4] the effects of which can be manifested at national as well as inter-personal levels. Where feeling, together with other inner processes of consciousness, is excised, models of human psychology become partial — the more 'objective' they become, the more they distance themselves from a lived sense of reality. Of behavioural psychology, in its extreme mechanistic stimulus/response state, Susanne Langer offered a crushing critique; for with its

> Idol of Objectivity [it] requires its servitors to distort the data of human psychology into an animal image in order to handle them by the methods that fit speechless mentality. It requires the omission of all activities of central origin, which are felt as such, and are normally accessible to research in human psychology through the powerful instrument of language. The result is a laboratory exhibit of behaviour that is much more artificial than any instrumentally deformed object, because its deformation is not calculated and discounted as the effect of an instrument.[5]

As an additional cautionary aside we may mention that attempts to make language itself fit the stimulus/response model of human behaviour must not only be partial, but wrong-headed, as Chomsky so decisively demonstrated in his refutation of B.F. Skinner's attempts to make language acquisition an elaborated system of operant conditioning.[6] For speech is not mere repetition or replication of elements of utterance previously-learned; utterance is a creative act. We do not simply 'respond' to stimuli. That would make us mere automata, reactors to that which acts upon us. We experience as an active condition of being, which is to say that we are experienc*ing* creatures — experiencing stimuli certainly, but not simply acted upon by them and thus shaped and determined by the nature and intensity of them. We are initiators also of our own behaviour. We are pro-active as well as reactive. Much of that impetus to the origination of behaviour springs from feeling — *our* feeling, which connects not simply to that moment, but potentially to the whole biography of our living, and is in no simple sense a causal response to immediate sensational stimuli.

It is feeling which in fact *prevents* us from making stereotyped and habitual responses, from acting in programmed ways. We attend to feeling when its power to attract and detain us makes us aware of something different or unique in our state of consciousness. Feeling calls attention of our selves to ourselves. If we fail to attend to feeling, or dismiss it, or learn habitually to ignore it, then we may lose our selves. For our 'powers of being' — of openness and receptivity — close until we have enclosed ourselves in a diminishing world of reality. Again, though well known, we ignore at our peril the testimony of Charles Darwin, reviewing late in life the career of his own sensibility. Having arrived at a point where he could no longer 'endure to read a line of poetry' and having 'also lost [his] taste for pictures and music' he knew, as Richard Hoggart expressed it, that 'something had withered in him'.[7] The evidence is in Darwin's own *Autobiography*:

> My mind seems to have become a kind of machine for grinding general laws out of large collections of facts, but why this should have caused the atrophy of that part of the brain alone, on which the higher tastes depend, I cannot conceive... If I had to live my life again, I would have made a rule to read some poetry and listen to some music at least once every week... The loss of these tastes (for one or more of the arts according to our predilections) is a loss of happiness, and may possibly be injurious to the intellect, and more probably to the moral character, by enfeebling the emotional part of our nature.

The Engagement of Feeling

Feeling is not, of course, the exclusive prerogative of literature and the arts. Any human activity may be invested with personal feeling — all branches of knowledge, pursuits and pastimes, hobbies, interests — almost anything we could list may engage the feelings of those who engage with them, and may be, in significant part, the reason why such individuals engage in those activities in the first place. Where the activity goes on, or must go on for extrinsic reasons, without any commitment of feeling, however, there may then be alienation of self. This is as true of the intellectual world as it is of the world of work. It is, for example, sadly true of several English Literature graduates I have met over the years. Their reading of literature has almost not involved them personally; certainly they have appeared to have no feeling for their studies, no excitement and no excitation of the senses in the literature they have studied. They seemed not to have been moved by poem or story, yet they have clearly performed the requisite analysis and exposition demanded of them in literary criticism. They had received creditable degrees, by dint of 'learning the tricks' and doing what was required. They might as well have studied the art of tree-pruning or the science of tarmacadaming. They might better have been employed, indeed, since in my meetings with them, they were preparing themselves as prospective teachers of English, and therefore of literature. I write of what I know. Colleagues tell me of teachers of History who have no interest in History, Science teachers who have no commitment to Science, and so on. Feeling is not engaged. Fortunately, the phenomenon is rare in the teaching profession, for we are surrounded by the children and older students with whom and with whose feelings we must also be concerned.

In the context of teaching literature, however, I think we are more crucially engaged with feeling and in ways which are additional to that of a feeling *for* a subject and the sense of excitement of being involved with it — a commitment of self we may develop productively towards any realm of knowledge and inquiry. For literary works, if they are to 'work', on us, must engage our feeling, just as the composition of literary writing involves us in a tapping of feeling. Both in the creative making of their own works and in the recreative activities of expressive criticism and appraisal of other writings, students research their own feeling, developing and refining awarenesses which they generate, adding to their stock of experience. They explore through feeling (not exclusively, but incompletely if excluded) the reality of their world and, through sympathetic extension, the worlds of others. The channels of feeling must be kept open for, as M.V.C. Jeffreys once reminded us, 'There is as much need for the education of feeling as for the education of thinking. The one cannot be left to chance any more than the other.'[8]

Feeling and Behaviour

Some behaviour corresponds immediately with the configuration of certain feelings. On such an occasion we 'feel what we are doing is right'. On other occasions we are aware of a dissonance, a dislocation between feeling and action which may in itself be disturbing. Something is not right. Reflection upon feeling, an introspective appraisal, may bring awareness of self and others. Most frequently we will articulate that feeling-state in the form of words, such as when 'talking things over' with others and of saying what one feels (which is often to *discover* what one feels). In the case of young children, their feelings can sometimes be diagnosed through close observation and interpretation of the patterns of their play. Psychotherapeutic counselling of adults, however, almost invariably would attempt, at some point, to help the individual towards verbal expression of whatever promoted the given disturbance, whilst other diagnostic activity-methods may contain, within themselves, a certain therapeutic value. It has long been recognized, for example, that informed study of paintings can reveal much of the individual's emotional complex. Whilst engaged in the painting itself the individual has experienced a reduction or dissipation of personal tensions through the activity. But such activity in itself does not lead to understanding; that requires of the individual a perception of the meaning somehow contained in or represented via the paintings made. By some means feeling must be transposed to cognition; it is to this movement from affect to understanding that we must direct attention wherever we attempt the education of feeling. The 'expression' of feeling alone does not suffice.

In the progression of our development feeling precedes intellect. We live by feeling before we learn to think in abstraction, as we live through the senses before we can confer meaning upon sensuous experience. Feeling and sensuous experience are the fundamentals of our being; they are and remain intimate with our biological being.

Forms and degrees of feeling operate as integers of virtually all human action. Feeling, the psychologist Klages asserted, is the integrative and cohesive aspect of all personality in the microcosm.[9] It is the source, Susanne Langer has extensively argued, from which those operations and performances of intelligence we ascribe to 'mind' are extruded and developed.[10] Feeling diffuses itself throughout action and thought; this is the elusiveness of our experience of feeling to which I have referred and to which the epigraph, the remark of D.H. Lawrence, similarly gestures.

The total reliance upon the promptings of feeling as the formulator of thought, attitude, and behaviour can mislead us. Lawrence himself — to whom Jung somewhere ascribed the faculty of what he called 'primitive thinking' — serves as an exemplar of this exaggerated response. Of his exposition to Lawrence of the Darwinian theory of evolution, and his exhortation to 'look at the evidence', Aldous Huxley records:

> His answer was characteristic. 'But I don't care about evidence. Evidence doesn't mean anything to me. I don't feel it *here!*' And he pressed his two hands on his solar plexus.[11]

An over-dependence upon personal feeling, unmediated by commerce with the world of other beings, may make social integration difficult. Jean-Jacques Rousseau's boast (or complaint), *'Je n'avais rien conçu; j'avais tout senti'*, indicates just such an inability to relate self to others. Rousseau's level of feeling and his attitudes developed from feeling-states, never matured. To a large extent he remained at that level of feeling promoted in him as a child, a result of sustained reading with his father of French romances of the seventeenth century. The effect of this early reading was to stultify his reason, confining him to that narrow range of feeling in which romance trades.

The dangers implicit in a heavy dependence upon feeling as the driving force of behaviour and expression are obvious. The acknowledgment should, however, remind us also of the fact that the products of rational-critical thinking can likewise provide us with erroneous thoughts and false ideas.

From Feeling into Words

Lawrence returned again and again to the preoccupation with feeling, both in his reflections and in his creative writings, where it formed one of the major endeavours of his artistic intention. 'We have no language for the feelings,'[12] he once complained, and his own insistent repetition, in the novels, of words like 'electric' and 'inchoate' indicates just such a language poverty for direct or literal *description* of meaning. In the art of literature it is only when words are creatively assembled that feeling is *embodied* — given an identity, 'a local habitation' if you like — and a sensuous charge given to action, picture, situation, event, circumstance, that it may be *presented*. When reduced to simple nominatives — joy, despair, love — complex feeling-states offer none of the particular lineaments of the occasion or of the summative expression of accumulated experience. Simple naming disperses and generalizes, making a category of reference which fails to take into account the individual character of the experience, and of feeling as the artificer of that response. Some of the critical reaction against the poems of Dylan Thomas might well start in the refusal to accept that such 'simple' feelings require such elaborate expression. What is overlooked in such judgments is the nature of those feelings themselves: feelings that can be but captured from moment to moment, not because they are rare or beyond ordinary experience (not in the least 'transcendental' or 'spiritual'), but because they are diffusive, evasively permeating the whole of experience, and frequently submerged. They are amorphous, not simply to be pointed at and immediately recognized. They are feelings woven through the texture of living itself. To be recognized they must first be recreated, *reconstituted*. Such artistic shaping leads us in turn to the 'complexity' of Thomas's poem 'The force that through the green fuse drives the flower ...'

We make poems (and other literature and art-forms) *because we can not otherwise say what it is we feel and think.*

There are times when, in the end and despite all our efforts, we still can not say. The poem remains as a history of the attempt to reconcile and transmute feeling into meaning. There is an exceptionally fine poem (much anthologized) by Thomas Blackburn which illustrates, more precisely than any other contemporary poem I know, just such an attempt to translate felt experience into 'sayable' meaning:

Hospital for Defectives

> By your unnumbered charities
> A miracle disclose,
> Lord of the Images, whose love
> The eyelid and the rose
> Takes for a metaphor, and today
> Tell to me what is said
> By these men in a turnip field
> And their unleavened bread.
>
> For all things seem to figure out
> The stirrings of your heart,

And two men pick the turnips up
And two men pull the cart;
And yet between the four of them
No word is ever said
Because the yeast was not put in
Which makes the human bread.
But three men stare on vacancy
And one man strokes his knees;
What is the meaning to be found
In such dark vowels as these.

Lord of the Images, whose love
The eyelid and the rose
Takes for a metaphor, today,
Beneath the warder's blows,
The unleavened man did not cry out
Or turn his face away:
Through such men in a turnip field
What is it that you say?[13]

Invoking the Lord of the Images, the god of Imagination, the experience is confronted. The heavy repetition of metre, the full rhymes, re-enact the insistent feeling. Uniquely a visual experience (like the language of the eyelid and the rose), the poem's images are released to explore the silences ('No word is ever said...'; 'The unleavened man did not cry out...') in the attempt to translate these 'dark vowels' into a language of sound, a language of *sense* ('What is it that you say?'). The disturbed feeling that the episode releases is embodied in the device of narrating the incident itself *and* of questioning it simultaneously. Yet the final articulation, of conceptual sense or understanding, eludes the very words which have been set free to capture it. Nonetheless, the disturbance persists, and is re-created as the artefact of the poem. The meaning, not of the poem, but of the experience recorded in the poem, remains obdurately wordless, inarticulate. It is experience at the limit of intellectual explanation. For, as in the example of Thomas Blackburn's poem, there are occasions when the closest we can get to some of the most profound of human experiences is in the pertinacity of the questions we ask and the precision of the form in which we put them. It is this act of poetic faith which has been woven throughout that symbolization which is the total poem.

Feeling can awaken our intelligence, our urge to *know*, even when such knowing can not issue in explanation. Feeling unites us with experience and gives us an immediate apprehension of the importance or significance of that experience to our selves. In this way we might say that feeling, whether in the event it leads us on in helpful fashion or misleads us, always has *value*. It is the affect of consciousness of which we are aware through the 'insistent self-reference inherent in feeling'.[14] The closer we can get to the particularization of what it is we feel, the more surely bonded may we become to the significance of our experience. The capacity to scrutinize feeling enables us to recognize our 'inner' world and discover in feeling its quality to confirm or transform the reality of experience. Feeling attended to can induce us to pay heed to such tacit awarenesses of self and so learn of one's self what it is one does value in the lived and living experience. The point can be demonstrated in the testimony of W.B. Yeats:

> ... when I re-read those early poems which gave me so much trouble, I find little but romantic convention, unconscious drama. But it is so many years before one can believe enough in what one feels even to know what the feeling is...[15]

Analysis of Feeling: Feeling as Perception

The theoretical origin and mechanics of the affective domain are still imperfectly understood, yet its phenomena, our everyday experience of being prompted to thought and action through feeling, can hardly be denied.[16] The difficulty of knowing what one feels and how one feels derives in large measure from the nature of the experience itself. For feeling is available to us only through introspection. We are aware of feeling only *through* feeling; we feel our feelings as experience. There is no laboratory specimen of feeling which we can analyze. Another measure of the difficulty we have in defining feeling derives from the nature of language in which we attempt the definition.

There are consensus meanings of words such as we find in dictionaries. But in a fundamental sense such meanings are the records of what we and others have done with those words — of what we have made them do. Words define themselves not by *de facto* operations of themselves upon the world of experience — they are not fashioned as *données* of nature over which we have no control — but rather as the world of experience has fashioned *them* through an inter-action with them.[17] Words signify by usage in context, in relation to other words and in relation to the 'sub-text' of ideas and associations with which they have been connected previously, according to their assembly within any given utterance.

In his linguistic analysis of the verb 'to feel' Gilbert Ryle identified seven uses, among others which he accepted might also exist.[18] He refers to a 'perceptual use' of feeling, 'in which we say that someone felt how hot the water was...' There is an 'exploratory use' in feeling for matches in a pocket or feeling a horse's legs. There is a 'mock-use' of feel when 'The condemned man already "feels" the rope around his neck, though there is not yet any rope around his neck...' Feel is used also 'in relation to aches, tickles and other local or pervasive discomforts'. Feeling may be used also to describe a general condition — such as feeling 'sleepy, ill, wide-awake, slack, fidgety, vigorous...' Additionally there is 'the very common usage in which we speak of feeling that something is the case ...' and of an interesting idiom 'in which we speak of feeling like doing something' ... (for example, to feel like laughing during the funeral service).

Ryle takes up in more detail the use of feeling that something is the case, or not:

When I feel that there is something amiss with an argument, I do not yet *see* what is wrong with it. If I did see what was wrong with it, then of course I could say what was wrong with it, and if I could say this, then 'feel' would no longer be the verb to use. 'Feel' goes with 'can't quite say.' (p. 284)

One, in passing, might add the rider that seeing what is wrong with an argument and saying what is wrong with it can not always be effected with the simple 'of course' transformation which Ryle implies. Sometimes only with great difficulty can one say what one sees. But what, it seems to me, is of more importance, is the reflection to which this use of 'feel' leads Ryle to assert:

Note that it is not the case of something being too delicate to be caught by our gross linguistic tools, but of its being too amorphous to be caught by our over-delicate linguistic tools. (Sometimes we say that an argument *smells* bad or that a promise *rings* untrue. Smelling and hearing are also inferior ways of perceiving. They warn us of things which we would prefer to have a good look at if only we could) (p. 284).

There are matters arising here which are in themselves worth having a good look at. Ryle's parenthetical comment that smelling and hearing are 'inferior' (to seeing) as ways of perceiving demands comment. Both smelling and hearing provide us with sensory information *simply not available through sight*. Each of our senses uniquely supplies experience. In language, through a case of synaesthesia, it is true that we do *express* one form of sensory experience through language belonging to another sense-mode (as in the examples Ryle himself offers). This in turn confirms the view I have offered of what we make language *do* in our attempts not merely to say, but to say with sensuous particularity; to convey not just 'meaning', but 'sense' — to suggest *how* an experience is to be apperceived rather than stating just the digest of its abstract. Even so Ryle has advanced an important observation to do with the over-delicacy of the instrument of language in its attempts to capture the phenomenon of feeling. For feeling *is* amorphous, diffused throughout the whole of our being, and the language in which we attempt our specifications slips past the nature of the object of our inquiry. (In another context of human experience, but with an appositeness to the present, a colleague once spoke to me of 'trying to measure a cloud with a pair of protractors'). Similarly diffused throughout the whole of Ryle's exposition of the linguistic usages of 'feeling', there is another point easily overlooked. It is that *all* of the usages cited by Ryle — not just that which he actually names 'the perceptual use' — imply modes of perception. As given, Ryle's examples of 'the perceptual use' refer to sensation, as do the 'aches and tickles' he mentions. Sensation similarly, though not in its entirety, is also involved in the 'general condition' of feeling 'sleepy, ill, wide-awake...'. These, and all other instances of feeling, convey vital information. The perception may be partial or incomplete, even vague, but without that first felt perception there would be nothing to go on. If we did not first feel that there was something amiss with an argument, we would have no reason to *want* to 'have a good look at it' to see what was wrong. If it did not 'smell' bad or 'ring' untrue, as we might say, we should presumably accept it as it is.

Perception, as I have expressed it before, is what we make of what we see, hear, touch, taste, or smell. Perception is also what we make of what we feel. What we feel, when the feeling is attended to, yields perceptions by which we know, in an appraisal of the information which we retrieve. We *know* we are sleepy or ill or wide-awake, because we have attended to what we are feeling — the evidences of our physiological and psychic state of the time. In periods when we are preoccupied with other matters, we sometimes do not recognize that we are in fact tired or unwell, simply because we have not attended to our feeling.

Enactments of Feeling

Feeling, often in advance of knowledge, advances knowledge. Feeling provides us with perception, which is as yet unformulated. The feeling may prompt immediate action. What we do directly expresses what we feel. When we 'do as we feel' feeling and behaving may be actually simultaneous — and sometimes virtually synonymous. In some teaching we attempt to get near to this experience when we first invite and then induce pupils to 'try out' certain feelings. Such an enactment of feeling must be central to any educational justification for the activities of role-play and improvisation in many areas of the curriculum, but crucially within literature and drama. In this context of role-play and improvisatory activities, though, I should perhaps add that the expression of feeling is not, *in itself*, a sufficient justification. What is learned *through* the activity (which is not the same as learning how to do something convincingly in an assumed role) must direct the objectives of the teaching. Of course this throws the methodological emphasis upon the need to devise sensitive 'debriefing' techniques following the activities, where some advocates seem to devote all their inventiveness to the devising of the role and situation briefs.

The enactment of feeling can, of course, take other and diverse forms. It may be sustained over a long period of time — as in artistic compositions in literature, dance, music, all the arts. In making a painting we may attempt to fix our perception of the initiating feeling; we then revise the painting as the feeling 'emerges', and then as we think about what we are doing, have so far done, we amend the visual representation. As the painting begins its embodiment, we interact with its emergence to discover that the conception which we can now begin 'to have a good look at' demands change. To the fashioning of the object we bring other disciplines of thought and technique; out of the medium itself, there may be suggested to us possibilities for incorporation — an accidental mix of paint could, for example, suggest just the right tonality for a segment of the canvas on which we work. We shall draw upon formal learning too, perhaps; from what we have learned about composition, arrangement, perspective, or we may employ, quite deliberately, traditional image or icon in the composition. As we proceed we may find the painting scavenging from other areas of experience from which we had not begun. The art object has begun to acquire — in a phrase used commonly by arts practitioners across all forms of making — 'a life of its own'. What I think this means is that at this point we now give our conscious attention to *it*, the object. At this stage the object sufficiently suggests the imprimatur of our feeling that we may turn away from the first impulse, or may hold it in abeyance, whilst we tend and minister and continue to shape the emergent form of the piece. To put the matter perhaps too simply, at this stage we perceive that the feeling is somehow 'there', projected onto the canvas in imagistic form. We have reached the stage at which, though the feeling requires further definition, we have done enough to locate the feeling in memory through the *aide memoire* of our painting. To recall the words of A.D. Hope cited in Chapter 3, having worked by habit and by trial and error, we now recognize the effect for which we were searching. We can at least see where we, and the painting, are going. We can now give our energies to working on the art, rather than working on the feeling; our continuing to work on the art itself suggests that we know we have not yet made, as precisely as we might, a representation of the felt reality towards which we began working. At some point we can do no more with the painting; if we have not overworked it, the painting is now finished. It is finished when, within its presentational form, we can see what it is that feeling has led us to know.

The characterization which I have offered here of art-making is simply illustrative. The history of the making of any one item of art will have its own individuality, but I am trying to suggest some of the experiential processes which operate within the matrix of art-making and which we can acknowledge. In these general terms, with particular extensions and refinements, which each of the arts and their practitioners would wish to offer, we can nonetheless see a certain connectedness. It is the transition from feeling to perception to cognition.

That is the movement, though it may not be, in each particular case (either of artist or individual work) the sequence of movement. I would accept that, in a given case, one may work from conception (an 'idea' of cognition), and then by working through the implications of that design connect with personal feeling in ways which then justify the formal properties of the initial conception. Determining the actual sequence in any one example is not my purpose; the movement is among and between feeling, perception, and cognition, in any order and degree, but all three are surely implicated in the making of any art. Immediately this offers us a very different model of art-making, and of arts activities, from that which views them as entirely subjectivist — the expression of feeling only, or such expression for its own sake. It challenges too the notion that all one has to do is simply to offer children the opportunity and encouragement to make art and they will do so. The view opposes the assumption that, as David Best put the point:

> ... the creation and appreciation of the arts is a matter of subjective feeling, in the sense of a 'direct' feeling, 'untainted' by cognition, understanding, rationality.[19]

Such a purist notion Best calls attention to in the work

... of theorists such as Witkin who wrote that in order to achieve this 'pure' feeling for art, one needs to erase all memories. The idea seems to be that cognition, understanding and memory will prejudice and limit the capacity for direct feeling-response; that they will prevent pure artistic feelings.[20]

In the making of art much more than the exclusive engagement of feeling is involved in the expression of feeling. There is the vital significance of memory in art-making. There is the matter of cultural forms, those indispensable means through which the artist may move towards the realization of art; and there are those occasions when the formal properties supplied by tradition enable the artist to identify the feeling in the first place, so that the individuality of personal representation may be begun. In engaging one's feeling a dialectic relationship is established; in some way one is necessarily trying to shape perception — to know what one should make of this feeling, how it affects one. Both in personal and educational terms this needs to be encouraged. It is vital in the process of self-realization, self-actualization, or whatever other term one would insert here to suggest that factor of psychic growth by which one comes to know oneself and others *personally*. Aesthetic activity must be given opportunity, of course; the purpose is to develop this pattern of growing awareness through the symbolization of art — one's own making, and that of others.

Feeling and Expressive Form

That feeling is a signal drive towards the composition of their art has been attested to by most artists from the so-called Romantic period onwards; Coleridge, Wordsworth, and Keats, for example. In *The True Voice of Feeling* Herbert Read collected a range of such testimonies.[21] He also gathered observations made by Hopkins, Yeats, Pound, and Eliot among others. Read, however, in a line of descendancy which one can hear echoed in the work of Robert Witkin, argues that the expression (or expulsion) of feeling will, in and through itself, supply the 'organic form' of the artwork in which state it will emerge. I doubt this. There is the issue, not only as to how we shall dispose ourselves towards the feeling, but also as to how to dispose ourselves towards the *conception* of the art form by which we hope to symbolize the feeling. In shaping the art we think of the art, not the feeling alone — whether or not one knows at the outset the eventual form towards which one is moving. There is the fact that feeling is not itself 'free-floating'. It must always refer to or derive from event or circumstance, the occasion of the feeling, to single experience or an accumulation of experience in which one was involved in a state of being. So almost certainly there will be the matter of what we think about the past. The expression of present feeling is not autonomous — it engages memory to test out the reality of experience which is our history.

To present feeling in any way encounters the limitations, as well as the potentials, of the medium in which one works towards a presentation or realization of the feeling. The medium imposes a necessary discipline. If this were not so, we could, working in the verbal mode, gather up all the words suggested to us as somehow implicated in the character of the feeling and then throw them at a piece of paper, as it were. There is all the difference in the world between 'automatic writing' and a poem. To compose a poem is unavoidably to shape experience. The words themselves are *not* the feeling; the poem is an orchestration of language which *symbolizes* the feeling, and the crafting of that symbol will engage attentions from us, which similarly are *not* the feeling itself. The place of feeling in the creating of the final form of the art object does persist, however, as that referent of experience against which the work-in-progress may be repeatedly checked and tested — and the cohesion of the piece around that feeling confirmed. Feeling will supply, too, that dominant mood or tone within which the work is conceived (feeling-on-the-way-to-understanding) which supplies the fulcrum or focus of the whole, or a passage in part. Whether, to recall again the words of A.D. Hope, we work by habit (through learned and systematic techniques), or trial and error (to discover the procedure for *that* occasion), the expression of feeling involves much more than involvement in and with the feeling alone. The making of the symbol, which then in some way *stands for* the feeling, is not achieved through 'free expression'. It is controlled expression; the instrument of control involves us in the reasoning out of what we have done, and what we are doing. Such reasoning matches the articulation of the work against the character of the feeling itself. This is so even where the intent is to exclude all which is extraneous to the matter of the feeling itself; the intent, for example, given by D.H. Lawrence:

> I have always tried to get an emotion out *in its own course*, without altering it. It needs the finest instinct imaginable, much finer than the skill of craftsmen.[22]

That complex of unformulated feeling-experience can be particularized and defined, as literature, only by subjecting experience to the control of language and to the form of the product made in language. Where one operates as if unaware of the control (acting 'unconsciously'), the shaping procedures are tacitly present in the feeling, or they could not be 'got out' as Lawrence puts it. This in turn sends us back to an investigation of the nature of feeling.

Feeling, Emotion, Knowing

Lawrence speaks of emotion. I have tended towards the generic 'feeling', to denote the affective domain of human experience. In many states of emotion there will be present to consciousness the effects of physiological sensation; these may also be present, in usually much reduced force, in states of feeling. Indeed, some psychologists, following William James,[23] have held that these sensations of physiological change *are* the emotion. One of the most helpful formulations of the distinction between sensation and feeling, however, holds that sensations, in fact, 'simply inform us what is there, while feelings *assess* what is there, including our own mental and bodily state'.[24]

Emotion is invariably charged with, or accompanied by, changes in breathing, pulse-rate, body temperature, and secretion. This is the physiological change to which sensations alert us. But an emotional state of being is not directed towards these effects. Though we may be aware of the effects, there is an object to the emotion. One is angry *at* something or someone, happy or in love *with* someone or something, or frightened *of* something. Emotion, in other words, is outgoing.

Most psychologists would now identify three interrelated features of emotion: the *conative*, the *cognitive*, and the *affective*. The conative impels us to action of some kind which can be contemporaneous with the emotional experience itself. Anger at someone or something, for example, is usually accompanied by and expressed through action as gesture, bodily attitudes and movement, and speech. The cognitive shapes a perceptual evaluation or understanding of the object of the emotion. We are angry at someone, *because* of our perception of his or her behaviour, attitude, or action. There is reason *in* our response of the moment, even if we fail adequately to express that reason, and whether, in the wisdom of after-the-event reflection, we or others deem our response 'reasonable' or 'unreasonable'. The cognitive element in emotion then makes us aware of the objects of our emotion; they are 'known' to us in ways which an 'emotionless' response could not develop. The conative element of emotion urges us to action, physical or mental. It is to feeling which the affective refers; feeling, simply, indicates to us how experience *affects* us. It is a qualitative assessment of experience, whether welcome or repugnant, the strength of feeling itself telling us how important or not something is to us. Feeling is the moderator of our sensibilities. Feeling is perhaps best viewed as that reflexive appraisal of self, inarticulate as we experience it in the moment, which disposes and discloses our inclinations. Within the outward-going response of emotion, there is also inwardly-directed feeling. It is possible, for example, to *be* angry (at someone else) and feel distaste (of oneself) for being so.

Feeling need not necessarily be attached to emotion on all occasions. But in all circumstances feeling evaluates experience by its appraisal of our total organic state. Feeling is psycho-physical: it provides us with awarenesses of our physiological state, through our apprehension of sensation, and of our mental states, through introspection. The attention to feeling is vital; it is a form of knowing. It is the means by which we come to know ourselves. It is in that realization of self that we engage with others, and encounter, so to enlarge and make richer, the reality of experience.[25]

Notes and References

1 Letter to Ernest Collings, 23/3/1914, in Huxley, A. (Ed.) (1932) *The Letters of D.H. Lawrence*, London, Heinemann, p. 182.
2 Mill, J.S. (1924) *Autobiography*, New York, Columbia University Press, p. 104.
3 Holbrook, D. (1961) *English For Maturity*, Cambridge, Cambridge University Press, p. 46.
4 Suttie, I.D. (1935) *The Origins of Love and Hate*, London, Peregrine, 1963.

5 Langer, S.K. (1967) *Mind: An Essay on Human Feeling*, Baltimore, Johns Hopkins University Press, p. 36.

6 Skinner, B.F. (1959) *Verbal Behaviour*, London, Methuen. Skinner's work, which had been published in America in 1957, was reviewed by Chomsky, N. (1959) in *Language*, **35**, pp. 26–58; the review is reprinted in Fodor, J.A. and Katz, J.D. (Eds.) (1964) *The Structure of Language: Readings in the Philosophy of Languages*, Englewood Cliffs NJ, Prentice-Hall.

7 Hoggart, R. (1970) *Speaking to Each Other*, 2, London, Chatto and Windus, p. 27.

8 Jeffreys, M.V.C. (1966) *Values in the Modern World*, revised edn., Harmondsworth, Penguin, p. 130.

9 Klages, L., 'The life of Feeling', in Arnold, M.B. (Ed.) (1968) *The Nature of Emotion*, Harmondsworth, Penguin.

10 Propositions which appear throughout *Feeling and Form* (1953) but which are most fully-developed in the sustained exposition of *Mind*, *op. cit.*

11 Huxley, A. (Ed.) (1932), 'Introduction', *The Letters of D.H. Lawrence*, London, Heinemann, p. xv. Despite the histrionic exaggeration of Lawrence's response, we might recall that as distinguished a scientist as Lord Kelvin said, of the Darwinian hypothesis of natural selection: 'I have *felt* that this hypothesis does not contain the true theory of evolution.' (Quoted by Harding, R.E. (1948) *An Anatomy of Inspiration and An Essay on the Creative Mood*, 3rd edn., Cambridge, Heffer, p. 97). Feeling-responses can seem to operate as a kind of 'affective intuition' in which we feel the value of something before there exists for us any rationalized grounds for believing something to be so. We may, in the event, be right or wrong so to believe.

12 Lawrence, D.H. (1961) 'The Novel and the Feelings', *Phoenix*, London, Heinemann.

13 Blackburn, T.E.F. (1978) *Selected Poems*, London, Hutchinson, p. 23.

14 Arnold, M.B. (1960) *Emotion and Personality*, 2 vols., New York, Columbia University Press, 1, p. 31.

15 Yeats, W.B. *Reveries Over Childhood and Youth*, quoted by Read, R. (1953) *The True Voice of Feeling*, London, Faber, p. 118.

16 Though the phenomena of feeling have themselves been disputed. The explanation of a class of affective phenomena known as 'emotions', according to a behaviourist methodology, can lead to such sophistries as: 'An Explanation of "Emotional" Phenomena Without the Use of the Concept "Emotion"'. (Duffy, E., a paper of 1941 reprinted in Arnold, M.B. (Ed.) (1968) *The Nature of Emotion*, Harmondsworth, Penguin).

17 The notion of Linguistic Relativity, advanced in the Sapir-Whorf hypothesis, argues that language *determines* thought. Most critics would reject the 'hard' version of the theory but accept its 'soft' amendment: that language *influences* thought. Whilst accepting this version as certainly so, I am simply pointing out that we can still make a word, or words, do novel things *in order to accord more closely with the nature of experience.*

18 Ryle, G. (1971) 'Feelings', in *Collected Papers 1929–1968*, II, London, Hutchinson, London, pp. 272–86.

19 Best, D., 'Feeling and Reason in the Arts: the Rationality of Feeling', in Abbs, P. (Ed.) (1989) *The Symbolic Order*, London, Falmer Press, p. 70.

20 David Best, *ibid*, referring to Robert Witkin's article 'Art in Mind: Reflections on *The Intelligence of Feeling*' in Condous, Howlett and Skull (Eds) (1980) *Arts in Cultural Diversity*, Sidney, Holt, Rinehart and Winston. Witkin's own book *The Intelligence of Feeling* (1974), in language at times obscurely theoretical, is nonetheless important in drawing attention to the value of feeling, and its place in art-making. David Best's alternative to the subjectivist view of Witkin will be

found more extensively treated in his *Feeling and Reason in the Arts* (1985), London, George Allen and Unwin. It will be clear from what I have so far outlined, in this and preceding chapters, that the 'interactionist view' (to give it a name) of feeling which I have adopted is closer to David Best's line of exposition than that of Robert Witkin's.

21 Read, H. (1953) *The True Voice of Feeling*, London, Faber.

22 From a letter to Edward Marsh, 18 August 1913, in *Letters*, *op. cit.*, p. 135.

23 The conflation of terms can be seen, for example, in James's paper (1884) 'What is an Emotion?', reprinted in Arnold, M.B. (Ed.) *The Nature of Emotion*, *op. cit.*

24 Arnold, M.B. *Emotion and Personality*, *op. cit.*, p. 31.

25 See Salmon, P. (Ed.) (1980) *Coming to Know*, London, Routledge and Kegan Paul, especially the essay by Miller Mair, 'Feeling and Knowing', pp. 113–27. Phillida Salmon herself, in her Introduction to this volume, usefully suggests that knowing 'blurs the edges' between thinking and feeling.

Chapter 6

From Impulse to Creative Formulation

> In the realm of the personal we move
> in invisible worlds, mostly private even
> from ourselves. In coming to know our-
> selves or others personally we will need
> to find ways to realize the invisible, to
> enter private worlds and get close enough
> to touch what hitherto we have refused to
> feel.
>
> Miller Mair[1]

First Promptings

The journey into the making of most works of literature, and most other art works too, is driven by feeling. It may not be the first impulse to the writing — that may have been supplied as an arresting idea which one has had — but the engagement with feeling is essential, if the work is to move towards completion. In his personal account of the making of a poem, referred to in Chapter 2, Stephen Spender speaks of 'a cloudy form of thought' or 'a dim cloud of an idea which I feel must be condensed into a shower of words' as his own experience of inspiration. Importantly, Spender immediately relates this kind of unformulated, or imprecise knowing, with feeling. It is feeling, the attempt to articulate how the experience affects him, which then supplies 'the pattern of sentience',[2] which gives cohesion to the final form of the piece. For the emerging composition, whose conception is at first only dimly perceived, is tested against the recollected feeling-response of previous experience. This is clear from Spender's further comments: referring to 'odd lines of poems written in note books fifteen years ago' he writes of the persistent nature of that memory for experience and of its essentially affective character:

> A few fragments of unfinished poems enable me to enter immediate-
> ly into the experiences from which they were derived, the circum-

stances in which they were written, and the *unwritten feelings* in the poem *that were projected but never put into words.*[3] (My italics)

Interestingly, in the compositional stage of working, Spender 'felt his way' (through twenty versions of a poem) towards a clarification of an imagined 'vision of the sea', the music of the language for that realization, *and* 'the inner feeling'. This is the reciprocity between inward experience and the object-in-the-making, towards which conscious attention must be paid, for the form of the art to issue.

In the context of that more expansive literary form of fiction, John Fowles wrote as follows of the inception of one novel:

> The novel I am writing at the moment (provisionally entitled *The French Lieutenant's Woman*) is set about a hundred years back. I don't think of it as a historical novel, a genre in which I have very little interest. It started four or five months ago as a visual image. A woman stands at the end of a deserted quay and stares out to sea. That was all. This image rose in my mind one morning when I was still in bed half asleep. It corresponded to no actual incident in my life (or in art) that I can recall, though I have for many years collected obscure books and forgotten prints, all sorts of flotsam and jetsam from the last two or three centuries, relics of past lives — and I suppose this leaves me with a sort of dense hinterland from which such images percolate down to the coast of consciousness.[4]

Here, again, one finds a confirmation of the possibility that the art-making itself connects with tracts of memory from one's world of experience — just as Livingstone Lowes in *The Road to Xanadu*,[5] showed the submerged memory of the poet in the making of Coleridge's 'Kubla Khan'. Fowles directs attention to something else important in his approach to this initial image of the woman — something which in general terms, though only a part of the whole matter, justifies our attempts to provide students with the possibilities of engaging with the products of their imagination and the imagination of others:

> I began deliberately to recall [the image] and to try to analyse and hypothesize why it held some sort of imminent power ...[6]

Imagination recasts elements of experience to make new potentials for experience. We direct conscious attention — training upon those products our mental powers of perception and cognition — in order that the encounter translates to a reality. Fowles's account illustrates the transition perfectly:

> The woman had no face, no particular degree of sexuality. But she was Victorian; and since I always saw her in the same static long shot, with her back turned, she represented a reproach on the Victorian Age. An outcast. I didn't know her crime ...[7]

Here one sees how the initial image grows, acquiring significance as the details of its perception accumulate and relate to other thoughts and ideas. The incepting idea requires a disposition of feeling towards it, if it is to grow. Fowles's admission proceeds:

> ... but I wished to protect her. That is, I began to fall in love with her. Or with her stance. I don't know which.[8]

What is clear, however, is that the growth of the emerging conception — the art product itself — makes demands of concentrated attention and draws upon resources 'outside of itself':

> Once the seed germinates, reason and knowledge, culture and all the rest have to start to grow it. You cannot create a world by hot instinct; but only by cold experience.[9]

Impulse to Making

There is deliberation in the making of literary forms. Without such control, subjective experience will not be objectified — made into a representation by which its significance may be apperceived. Hence the stressing of feeling, rather than emotion, as the impulsion towards meaning. During the immediacy of an emotional experience we find articulation difficult; we are overwhelmed by the direct symptoms and expressions of the emotion. Grief-stricken, we cannot say how we feel; speechless with rage, we cannot identify the character of the cause, the particularities of the occasion traced through their connections with history — *why* we rage. In some way the spontaneity of emotion conflicts with the urge to *make sense* of that experience. It is in this reason that we find, I believe, a new significance in Wordsworth's famous account of the origins of his own poetry as detailed in the Preface to the second edition of *Lyrical Ballads* (1800):

> ... it takes its origin from emotion recollected in tranquillity till by a species of reaction the tranquillity disappears, and an emotion, kindred to that which was before the subject of contemplation, is gradually produced, and does itself actually exist in the mind.[10]

The notion of poetry as simply 'the spontaneous overflow of powerful feelings' has already been challenged — and Wordsworth's fuller description suggests something else. The *impulse* to the making of the poem is in the feelings which persist and which are derived from the initial emotion — and which, through active contemplation recreate, as it were, the 'after-effect' of emotion itself. Something of this sense is implicated in Robert Graves's account of the active recalling of affective experience — the contemplation of the emotion preceding the 'secondary phase', as he calls it, of the act of composition itself:

The nucleus of every poem worthy of the name is rhythmically formed in the poet's mind, during a trance-like suspension of his normal habits of thought, by the supra-logical reconciliation of conflicting emotional ideas. The poet learns to induce this trance in self-protection whenever he feels unable to resolve an emotional conflict by simple logic.[11]

Literary composers must use their own language by which to attempt an exploration into and description of their own creative processes, and Graves's use of 'trance-like' to refer to the preparatory stage of writing might seem an oddity to some readers. In one way or another, though, there is within all of us experience which is somewhat compatible — though not, perhaps, quite so fully-blown as to be akin to a trance. Whenever we concentrate fully on a given task, there is an integration of personality directed towards that accomplishment. The object of our task draws from us those energies and that thinking required for the fulfilment of the object; our other capacities and energies are suppressed or ignored in order that the concentration may proceed. 'The rest of the world', as one might commonly express it, must be ignored. To shape a work of art we must in some fashion shape ourselves towards *it*.

Rosamund Harding, from her extensive inquiries into the working habits of a wide range of creative makers and thinkers, came to the following conclusion. There is a creative 'mood', a total psycho-biological orientation of the maker, which somehow contains within it, and will suggest other, materials required for the making of the object:

The mood induces concentration which focuses the mind on the conception and it attracts ideas suitable to the expression of the conception. The conception is the form of the piece and the mood is the key system.[12]

It is this mood which enables us to tap the entire resource of consciousness, those possessions of memory held in pre-conscious or unconscious states, as well as those contents 'known' to us in ready awareness. All creativity brings something into being which did not previously exist. Artistic creation brings into being something of ourselves, including at times what might have been suppressed or repressed, but somehow held inferentially within the gestalt of our conception. The art object, the object of our concentration of effort, stands as a representative symbolization of that integration of personality demanded of us for the realization of *its* character.

Creative Formulation

There are some striking similarities between the accounts of the creative encounter with the reality of experience and Carl Jung's exposition of a diagnostic activity-method which he developed. Outlined in an essay called 'The Transcendent Function',[13] written in 1916, but not published until 1957, the method aims at 'the union of conscious and unconscious contents' through 'the complementary attitude' of the latter towards the former. Since the conscious and unconscious are often in opposition, it is first necessary to get access to the unconscious material in order to 'supplement' the former. The whole endeavour concentrates on 'the question of meaning and purpose'. The procedure focuses on the 'active imagination', and consists essentially of the following: by immersion in the mood and the attempt to make oneself 'as conscious as possible of the mood [one] is in' or 'the emotional disturbance' one is experiencing, the individual records 'all the fantasies and free associations that come up'. These, Jung notes, may be put down on paper as notes, or drawn as images, or worked in a plastic material. At this stage 'critical attention must be eliminated'. An intellectual analysis of what one is producing would hinder the release of the images one is seeking, the 'free fantasies' offered up through the active imagination.[14]

To this 'more or less complete expression of the mood', the material in verbal, pictorial or plastic form representing the free fantasies, the individual will respond, Jung suggests, in one of two typical ways. One will aim at *creative formulation*:

> Where the principle of creative formulation predominates, the material is continually varied and increased until a kind of condensation of motifs into more or less stereotyped symbols takes place. These stimulate the creative fantasy and serve chiefly as artistic motifs. The tendency leads to the aesthetic problem of artistic formulation.[15]

The other will aim at *understanding*:

> Where ... the principle of understanding predominates, the aesthetic aspect is of very little interest and may occasionally even be felt as a hindrance. Instead, there is an intensive struggle to understand the *meaning* of the unconscious product.[16]

There is danger in using either response exclusively. In the intellectual analysis of the material the symbolic character of the product may be lost; in the aesthetic, 'the real goal of the transcendent function may become sidetracked into the problems of artistic expression'. In proportion, however, the two tendencies complement each other, since attempts at intuitive understanding of the material may be erroneous when the material itself has not been sufficiently shaped, and over-shaping may take the material away into regions of experience other than those from which it originated. It is in the shuttling to and fro between argument and a statement of how the material *affects* one (one's feelings towards the material itself) that the transcendent function reconciles those opposites of the tension which first gave rise to disturbance.

There is an interpenetration of art-making and understanding. The understanding is somehow *in* the making itself. It is sometimes not until that making has achieved a certain status, a recognizable realization of form, that one can begin to penetrate to the tacit formulation of understanding inherent within its construction. The making of literature can not, ultimately, be disassociated from the movement towards understanding, however imperfectly expressible that understanding might be when we attempt its statement in intellectual terms, and however the work itself eludes a completely satisfying 'paraphraseable' equivalent. Indeed the value of literature is that it achieves a symbolizing inclusiveness of meaning and experience which necessarily exceeds the linear representation of any argumentative or discursive line of exposition. It is something to be borne in mind constantly that the effect of literature includes something other than, as well as something more than, the explicit formulation of exegetical criticism.

Promoting Literary Writing: Preliminaries

In examining these accounts of the transformation of the world of experience into literary form, we can begin to indicate some of the processes involved in that act of creation. Knowledge of these processes will not in itself, of course, yield a secure means of progressing either in our own writing or in the promotion of literary writing with our students. Nor do the insights offered by writers translate the processes of literary writing into a set of *skills*. We can not, in any case, separate skills from that act within which they are deployed. Nor does the promotion of literary writing gain anything from a knowledge of the personal idiosyncrasies of established writers. It helps us not at all to know that Trollope insisted on his daily three thousand words, or that Hemingway thought a good day's work to consist of three hundred — that Trollope wrote sitting down, that Hemingway wrote standing up. Or that Dickens insisted upon his desk being aligned north to south, and that Vladimir Nabokov wrote always in pencil. Yet these idiosyncrasies of composition must be allowed for, of course, so far as they may be in classroom or workshop. One can not legislate for those personal conditions within which the creative condition is most likely to be productive.

The writing we seek to promote should serve a literary function and will achieve literary form. It will be expressive, directed through the functions of art-making, and working towards forms which connect with genre and the traditions of culture — all of which are actively explored, not imposed as restriction. For each experimentation will itself prove the validity of form and the necessity of limits.

The value of the enterprise is two-fold. First, that our students should have access to means by which they can come to know personally, to explore and to realize the realities of their own experience. Second, so that through this making, they have surer means of access to other works of literature; means by which they can attend to these works, respond and appraise them as extensions of the world of experience. The writings which they produce may not be achieved works of art in their own right, and many will confine themselves to realizations which are intensely personal. Nonetheless, I believe, such writing acts as intermediary to the literary experience.

What follows is by no means held up as ideal practice, and it is certainly not intended as an inventory of 'techniques' by which to encourage art-making. It is notional, attempting to illustrate bases upon which good practice may be founded.

Stimulus — Focus of Attention — Engagement

It perhaps seems redundant to begin with the observation that, if writing is to proceed, there must first be an *impulse* to create, to write. This is a recognition of the desire or need to give shape to aspects of experience. The need can not be artificially induced, but it can be encouraged. It is encouraged through a connection of consciousness attending to experience so that the person wishes to dwell in that experience — to examine, to explore, to reflect. Sometimes, when we are lucky as promoters of the literary experience, that impulse is there already; though even here we must offer more than mere opportunity for expression, because the direction and eventual form of that impulse in most cases will benefit from sensitive proposing and negotiating of possibilities within which experimentation may begin. There are times when we help the student to see the nature of that towards which the impulse is directed so that experience may be engaged, and its character thereby more closely delimited in the exploratory writing which follows. Given such a sense of direction, the student is then free to improvize among the means by which the impulse may be articulated — the literary conception enabling experience to be accommodated. In these and other instances we can help the student towards aspects of genre or form or style through which to shape and realize the conception which will emerge from the impulse to create.

Most often, however, we will need to provide some means by which to activate that impulse. Here we offer a *stimulus* to awaken or develop an impulse to compose. The stimulus itself can take almost any form, be of almost any kind: objects, sensory impressions (as in tape-recordings of various sounds), poems or other literary writings, pictures, narrations ... the potential listing of priming material is endless. Of course one selects according to one's view of what is likely to succeed with a given group of students, but not in any instrumental way which will guarantee a 'ready made' response. In fact, that is the very opposite of what we seek to promote. Ready-made response is cliché or formula. We wish to promote first-hand language — which is why, in the beginning of a scheme to encourage literary writing, my own practice has been to use non-verbal material as the stimulus. It is a surer way, I believe, to avoid the derivative.

What matters, though, is not the mere presentation of the object (*stimulus*), but the ways in which one promotes *engagement* of the individual with that stimulus. The deficiency in some procedures is that the stimulus is all that is offered. Art-making is not equivalent to the reductionist stimulus-response model of human behaviour — 'I'll show you a picture, now you write a poem.' Many students will still not be able to begin because, they say, they have nothing to say. There is no engagement; no perceptual, cognitive, affective connection of individual with the object which constitutes the stimulus. To put it simplistically, the object has not become an experience for the individual. There has been no subjective extension of self.

Expression is never free; it is always tied to experience of which it is an outcome. In order that the stimulus may become experience for the student, we may have to provide a *focus of attention* — means, devices, processes through which the individual can apprehend the object or stimulus, and be drawn subjectively towards the qualities of its inherent nature. Through such a focus of attention we are, in effect, indicating possible ways in which to 'see' the object, showing the students how they may address themselves to it. Through that, there is greater likelihood that the individual will discover the relationship between self and object; it is precisely that space between self and object which the literary writing will occupy.

I shall illustrate these processes with examples which feature visual stimuli. Within a class of first-year secondary school pupils one group of children had been invited to look at a print of a stone relief carved on a wall of a temple in Cambodia. To engage them with the object I directed attention first by inviting them simply to write down the details of the features of the carving, which immediately struck them on looking at the picture. Together they noted some of the details of the representation — gods, snakes, shields, for example. The students made their own jottings. They looked again individually at particular details of the relief, at my suggestion to see if any of them connected with other features of the carving, but without telling them that the carving was a symbolic narrative. They were then to tell me what they thought of what they had seen. In brief, the stimulus (the print) was scrutinized, not just presented, through devising ways in which the students would actually have a good look at what was there. Seeing these matters then connected with personal thought and feeling. Here is one of the poems made:

The Statue

> The man who carved this statue
> Must have had blood shed
> In his mind,
> Because of the shields,
> Poisonous snakes,
> And ragged robes.
> The snakes bite poison
> Into the gods' veins.
> The giants fight
> The gods.
> And the gods fight
> The giants.

Ivor Watkins

Interestingly the boy's 'conclusion', in the making of the poem, is stated first — though it was to this he had been led, as it were, from the reconstruction of his own selection of detail from the carving, and his perception of some of the narrative elements of the original. The focus of attention by which we enable students to engage personally with the stimuli may not need to be elaborate at all. Here it was simply in the form of suggestive questions (the question pointing to narrative features in the original design, for example, was simply: 'Do you think this has got anything to do with that?' — whilst the moving finger pointed). Without being ready with a focus of attention through which students can engage with the stimulus, we run the risk of no response at all.

Sometimes our students can not see anything because they are looking at everything.[17] The focus of attention enables them to look with a proper regard. It does not confine them to the perceptions carried in that focus; rather it frees them to see personally. One of the girls in that class of eleven-year-olds produced the following:

The Temple

In the temple
Carved on a wall
Are pictures of men
Brave and tall
with spears
In their hands
Fighting, fighting
For their lives.

Susan Wood

With this, her very first poem, Susan (who was very clear about the intention and said so) experimented with the shape of the poem in an attempt to convey something of the three-dimensional effect of the wall carving — the sense of relief carried in the indented lines.

A further example of the potential importance of devising a focus of attention through which to engage with the stimulus offered will indicate another of its possible forms. In this case the stimulus offered was a colour reproduction of Edward Hicks's 'The Peaceable Kingdom'; again it is drawn from the teaching of a first-year secondary school class. After initial observation of the print the students were presented with this focus of attention — the passage from *Isaiah*, 11, vv. 6–9, beginning: 'The wolf also shall dwell with the lamb, and the leopard shall lie down with the kid...' The passage was explored, through discussion, for what it might mean, and a few personal jottings made. This attention — a range of possibilities — was then redirected to the painting. One of the boys produced the following poem:

Fable

It happened one day
When a lion fell in a stream.
And the animals shouted 'Oh, my king!'
The ox jumped in with a terrible splash,
And pulled out their precious king.
Then the lion said 'Let there be peace with man and beast'.

The bear was feeding with the bull,
And children
Playing upon their backs,
And people having a friendly chat.
The tree was changing colours very quickly,
And the stream flowed by so clear
On that happy day.

Welcome to the land of peace —
And see for yourselves how peaceful it is.

Andreas Ioannou

Gathering and Forming

In all of these examples I have mentioned, in passing, another process in the passage towards the literary product — that of making notes or jottings. In fact, this is a critical stage in the progress, and I think of it as the process of *gathering*. Gathering, in its initial form, is a collection of impressions of aspects of the stimulus — observed details, images, significant information about the object — and a collection of one's responses to those impressions of the object: what and how one thinks and feels about these matters in relation to one's self. This latter aspect may then induce recollection of previous experience, associations with other experience which is not of the moment of one's contemplation of the object itself. Gathering is thus both inwardly-directed, to self and memory, and outwardly-directed, to the object. Such a gathering of impressions is the beginning of the identification of that space which the artwork will occupy, uniting objectivity and subjectivity in that third dimension where art works. The gathering enables identification of what is significant to self in relation to the object of one's contemplation, reflection, and disposition of feeling. From such noting of key images, phrases, connections and contiguities the process of *creative formulation* takes its shape.

Gathering is not the same as rough-drafting — the first and subsequent attempts to embody these perceptions within the conception of the piece as it begins to appear. The suggestiveness of the gatherings becomes some kind of tacit inherence of the direction which the impulse to create will follow. Mature writers might, on occasion, do without a hard copy of their gatherings; they do not require a paper version, since the gathering might be simultaneous with the drafting and redrafting. They gather as they write. But in educational contexts a physical gathering actually confirms for the student that there is 'something there' to begin with and from.

Gatherings may take the form of 'making notes', but that description would belie their significance. Sometimes, with my teachers-in-training, to demonstrate this stage of gathering, I invite them to participate in the following activity. I hold up a candle. It is an ordinary, white, household candle, and an initial focus through which, by suggestive prompting I ask them to think of a particular candle they have in mind (that is, retrieved from memory) and to note briefly any of its characteristics: colour, size, shape, whether newly-lit or guttering, the cast of light . . . etc. Then I say that the candle must be on or in something; and notes are again made — though even from the first promptings one or two students have made sketches rather than verbal records. The candle occupies a certain location: room, church, club... There is a person or persons especially connected with this location... Is there a particular event which you associate with this person, these persons, the location, and the burning or the lighting of that candle? . . .

The candle, in this demonstration, is really simply a prop, though even so, it does act as some kind of stimulus — something one can look at in that unnoticing way when one's attention is actually directed elsewhere — to the evocation of memories. The focus of attention is in the questioning and prompting. Spaces of time between each prompt allow for personal connections with memory to be established; the jotting of detail and image, which in turn enable further recollection to be made. More time still is made available, when the prompt questions are at an end, for each individual to recall and record related associations, operating directly now from her or his own notes, which are then supplemented in whatever way the student chooses.

Students are often surprised at how much they can recall, and the detail in which they recall it. The impulse to create, to shape their jottings into a fuller record, has invariably accompanied this recognition of memory. I suggest they might shape a piece of writing, which will take the form of memoir, or to use the details of their own recollected experience to shape into a passage of impressionistic writing.

Here is one example of the writing which emerges. It was written by a mature woman, who said that until this occasion she had forgotten all about the incident. Nonetheless, she spent the evening of that day completing the writing, to get as close to the experience as possible. Later she told me that the writing had enabled her to perceive more fully the nature of her family relationships through the recall, in its significant detail, of this episode from many years ago. (Since the writing was subsequently displayed unsigned I shall preserve that anonymity.)

The Candle

Our first christmas as a married couple — we had so looked forward to it. Are there, however, any married couples who do not have to debate annually how, and more importantly where Christmas is to be celebrated?

Foolishly, we decided to open our house to both his parents and mine, at this special christmas time. In retrospect it was a recipe for disaster, if ever there was one.

His parents, home owners, fairly 'well-heeled', fitted neatly into the lower middle class. His father was a man to be reckoned with — a NATSOPA no less! My parents fitted even more neatly into the lower working class bracket. Council house tenants. Dad was a dust cart driver, unskilled you see, and my mother? She was a semi-literate office-cleaner, and she knew her place.

Undaunted or perhaps desensitised by the excitement and planning, I went ahead with my christmas preparations. The Christmas Pudding recipe I used (for the first time) was a family one, almost a hundred years old. This was indeed to be 'a traditional family christmas'.

Christmas morning passed without incident, everyone was making an effort, but the differences in personalities and perceptions were apparent, even then.

Lunch was well under way. I began to set the table, whilst my husband hosted the families. A new crisp, white damask table cloth was quickly covered with red linen place settings and table napkins. The cutlery and crystal glasses shone in the artificial fluorescent lighting. My *pièce de résistance* was a table decoration — a yule log, adorned with tiny pine cones and red ribbons. It was surmounted by a red, twisted candle. I stepped back with some satisfaction to admire my handiwork. Yep! it looked good.

Lunch was to be served. I called out to the family a 'five minute warning'.

I lit the candle. Flickering candles always touch heavily upon my emotions at christmas. His mother came into the dining room first. 'That looks nice dear!' I smiled appreciatively — his father followed — then came my mother — looking slightly uncomfortable. The candle flickered as the bodies moved and settled into their chairs. My husband now at the head of the table sat, surveying the scene.

Enter, my father. The candle spluttered, red wax began to run slowly, but stopped at the first twist in the bright red tallow. My father pulled his chair noisily toward the table, nodded at the candle and said, 'You expectin a bleedin' pow'r cut then gal?'

This is personal writing; the intensity of the personal recollection of an experience which occurred many years in the past is clearly evidenced here. Such personal writing justifies itself for the person — thus the promotion of such personal writing, within the educational context, justifies itself, too, as a contribution towards the essential aim of self-realization. But one can see, from this example, how such writing shapes itself towards a literary form — already it is close to being a short story in its own right. It is as if the nature of the experience demanded narrative for its expression. As is the case with literary writing, there is a fund of implicitness here. One can readily see, for example, how the formulation 'Enter, my father' is saturated with sense (to refer back to matters posed in Chapter 4) and proposes also its own sense of anticipatory drama.

From the stage at which gatherings are made proceeds the creative formulation itself — the making and shaping. Here is a complex of activity which refers essentially to the processes of experimentation and improvisation through which we move towards the form of that particular piece of literary writing — including notions derived from other examples of form within the genre. Shaping implies selection, elaboration, refinement, questioning, the search for alternatives — all of that psychic activity of thinking, feeling, sensing, and intuiting by which we move through drafting and redrafting of the work-in-progress towards its final form.

Implied within the making of this final form is the constructor's own attitude towards the work — an appraising of the work itself, for what it enables the writer to come to know. To the composer this is a critical attitude towards both the embodied meaning of the piece and the extent to which the final form is an adequate realization of that direction of meaning. It is predicated in the initial impulse to create the work in the first place. The working towards the final form is thus not 'thoughtless'. The maker, in the making, develops a critical attitude towards the work; coming to know, in the sense in which I have characterized this movement towards understanding, is invariably tied to judging.

With all that creative formulation implies, the process ends in the production of the final form of the work, the art product. It has achieved its own identity.

Aesthetic Approach: Formal Study

With that identity we have arrived at the end of the interactive continuum resulting in the final form of the students' own literary writings. We have not, however, completed all the processes involved in the conception of a literature-within-the-arts, of a literary education which attends to the full range of aesthetic potential. To complete the cycle we must attend to the matter of *presenting* the literary work to others, and to those activities which are involved in formulating what we might think of as *responding* and *evaluating*. These will, within an aesthetically-conceived view of literature-teaching, be different in some ways from what we are used to thinking of as the critical response. To these matters I turn in some detail in Part III of this book. But I should like to conclude here with a further illustration of the processes of stimulus, focus, engagement, gathering, and impulse with which I have so far been occupied — through a more elaborate, and certainly more achieved poem. I shall point to these processes as they were involved, in a more attenuated, more integrated fashion, in the creative formulation which produced the final work. It will demonstrate not only something of the literary writing of which students are capable, but will also give the lie to those who do not see how this aesthetic approach can find its place within the formal study of literature. It shows quite clearly, I believe, the advantages of working *in* literature to promote work within the total aesthetic field of literature, including that of intellectual criticism.

In the course of a GCE 'A' Level programme one of the areas of study prescribed for the students was that of the poetry of the First World War, with set texts drawn from the work of Owen, Sassoon, Brooke, and others. In this case, it was the poems themselves which were the stimulus to a shaping of personal response through literary writing. In large measure the student discussions provided the focus of attention, in that these enabled the students to realize what they thought and felt about the matters presented in the poems, to reflect more generally on the issues proposed in the individual texts — the procedures of 'art-speech' by which one comes to know personally through works of art. The focus was supplemented by particular additions: a viewing of the film *All Quiet On the Western Front*, for example, and the reading of selected information about the First World War, including that of the 'Christmas Truce' on the Western Front, during which time the opposing armies fraternized with each other. Throughout their study of these texts I had encouraged the students to keep what I have here called a gathering: of notes, images, reflections, ideas, and responses, which at some point might be shaped into a summative expression of their experience of the poetry in literary writing, a poem, or a 'collage' narrative. This personal gathering was frequently derived from other notes made to each of the studied texts. The re-creative act of exploring textual meaning combined with the creative act of first-making. The students' own literary writings, when completed, were collected and then presented within the class, so that they, too, became objects of study, reanimating further inquiries into the set texts. In presenting their own writings within the group, the students also tracked, so far as possible, their individual progression from set texts to personal created form — noting the connections, associations, contiguities and differences among and between the poems studied and their own text. Other students also made suggestions from their response to individual poems. The presentation of their own writings thus acted as a means by which students could *re*-engage with the texts set for formal study.

Here is one of the poems which was presented:

Christmas Eve

Wet mud, congealed blood, mixed and used
As face packs.
Death comes down our mausers and
Lee Enfields bearing gifts of sleep.
Second anniversary of futility and
Senseless destruction, there is something we lack.
At night I squirm from the touch
Of rats and man, and weep.

Something happened on this day a long
Time ago in Bethlehem.
The order of the child massacre by
Lord Protector, Herod of Galilee.
There is no difference between his order
And the ones given by them.
A light, a flame, a candle, something bright,
What is it I see?

Kamarade, share my bully and I will
   drink your schnapps.
Arm in arm, brothers of the night,
   hid from these Bastards' sight,
We celebrate together; Together. Together
   and laugh, and sing, and pray.
God give us your mercy and hold
   back tomorrow's light.
Back, retreat, the mad hounds bay out orders,
Their screaming minds do not understand this situation.
Merry Christmas.

Stewart Stark

Notes and References

1 Mair, M., 'Feeling and Knowing', in Salmon, P. (Ed.) (1980) *Coming to Know*, London, Routledge and Kegan Paul.

2 A phrase of Keats, quoted by Read, H. (1953) *The True Voice of Feeling*, London, Faber and Faber, p. 153.
3 Spender, S. (1946) 'The Making of a Poem', *Partisan Review*, 13, p. 303.
4 Fowles, J., 'Notes on an Unfinished Novel', in Malcolm Bradbury (Ed.) (1977) *The Novel Today*, London, Fontana, pp. 136–50.
5 Lowes, J.L. (1959) *The Road to Xanadu*, New York, Vintage Books.
6 Fowles, *op. cit.*, p. 136.
7 *Ibid.*
8 *Ibid.*
9 *Ibid.*, p. 138.
10 In Hutchinson, T. (Ed.) (1969) *Wordsworth: Poetical Works*, Oxford, Oxford University Press, p. 740.
11 Graves, R. (1949) 'The Poetic Trance', in *The Common Asphodel*, London, Hamish Hamilton, p. 1.
12 Harding, R.E. (1948) *An Anatomy of Inspiration and An Essay on the Creative Mood*, 3rd. edn., Cambridge, Heffer, p. 123.
13 'The Transcendent Function', in (1960) *Collected Works*, VIII, London, Routledge and Kegan Paul, pp. 67–91.
14 *Ibid.*, pp. 69, 75, 78, 82–3.
15 *Ibid.*, p. 84.
16 *Ibid.*
17 In the context of visual materials (prints and photographs) used as stimuli, I have found the following simple device unfailingly acts as a physical means to a focus of attention, with young and mature students alike. I hand it on for what it might be worth to others. It consists simply of two L-shapes cut out of cardboard — and the students can make them for themselves in seconds:

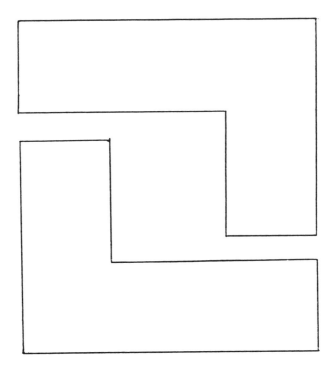

The two cut-outs can then be moved, one over the other, to make any number of rectangles of different sizes and shapes. These 'frame' different aspects of the composition shown on print or photograph. By moving around these frames students will discover details they had not registered — and teachers can direct perception to particular features of note.

Part III

The Aesthetic Field of Literature: Text and Context

In their own expressive writings, students engage directly with the realities of personal experience. Such writings may also explore the properties and traditions of literary form, and may engage with the literary experience of other texts. The reading of literature becomes a collaborative venture in the re-making of meaning through personal, and shared, responses to a text. Those responses are perceptual, affective, and aesthetic, as well as intellectual — and involve an immediate sensuous apprehension of the effects of the work. Providing access to such responses focuses attention on the manner in which each literary work is presented. Providing opportunities for the articulation of such responses, similarly, may be effected through the students' own active experimentation with presentational form. Expressive activities in their own right, such presentations induce reflection and interpretation, whilst enabling further connections to be made to other disciplines within the community of arts. Creative involvement and critical enterprise proceed together towards comprehension and understanding. Text and the context of experience encounter each other: in this contemplative understanding new realities may be proposed and judged.

Chapter 7

Reading and Response:
Response and Presentation

> The *product* of art — temple, painting,
> statue, poem — is not the *work*
> of art. The work takes place when
> a human being cooperates with the
> product so that the outcome is an
> experience that is enjoyed because
> of its liberating and orderly properties.
>
> John Dewey[1]

The Aesthetic Field: A Summary

It might provide a useful reference-point to offer here a schematic summary of the creative and re-creative processes of the aesthetic field of literature, before proceeding to related matters. Though schematic, I do not intend this to be taken as mechanistic, and some essential qualifications need to be borne in mind. Within the following outline, which takes up the terms of reference offered in the preceding chapter (stimulus, focus, engagement, gathering, impulse and formulation), the stages of progression are shown from stimulus onwards, ending with the students' own literary writings. The full progression through the aesthetic field of literature, however, would go beyond this stage of production, and lead towards evaluation. The purpose, in the sequence which follows, is to show that the conventional aim of literature-teaching, to end in discursive criticism, may not necessarily leap directly from the stimulus of the text to the talking or writing about it, which makes the critical evaluation.

The order of these 'events', as shown, is therefore notional, in the sense that on any given occasion the order may change, indeed should change, but the activities and operations which they represent will nonetheless be present. Clearly, there are other points at which one might begin in the movement through the full aesthetic field. Each stage is defined by *purpose* not by activity: the same activity may be used to promote different outcomes — to enter and to re-engage with the aesthetic field at different points. Thus, notionally and in practice, there are different routes which these processes may take, and different points-of-entry, where each stage might operate. Additionally, some stages in the sequence feed back into each other, and some operations may go on simultaneously, rather than as separate and unrelated phases. They are all, nonetheless, involved in the full movement of the literary enterprise founded on creative principles. Such points of reference may help us to design lessons intended to lead students into the experience of literature as art:

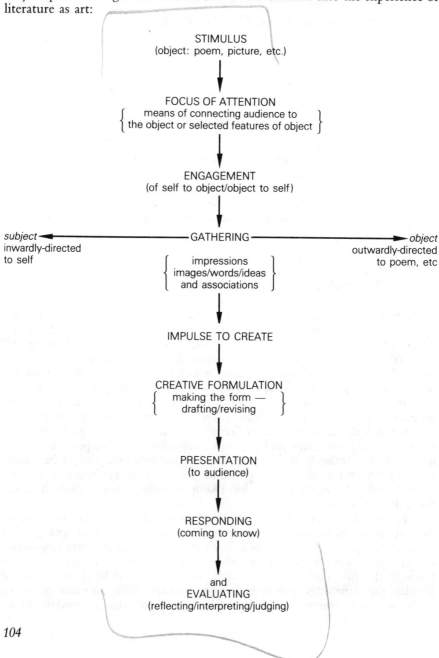

STIMULUS
(object: poem, picture, etc.)

↓

FOCUS OF ATTENTION
{ means of connecting audience to
the object or selected features of object }

↓

ENGAGEMENT
(of self to object/object to self)

↓

subject ◄———————————— GATHERING ————————————► *object*
inwardly-directed   outwardly-directed
to self   to poem, etc

{ impressions
images/words/ideas
and associations }

↓

IMPULSE TO CREATE

↓

CREATIVE FORMULATION
{ making the form —
drafting/revising }

↓

PRESENTATION
(to audience)

↓

RESPONDING
(coming to know)

↓

and
EVALUATING
(reflecting/interpreting/judging)

The final step, the evaluation, looks back to the original stimulus; in fact, all of the processes along the way refer in some way to this initiating point of the whole literary progress. If the student presents work to an audience, its presentational mode may well differ from its written form. An obvious example of this is the saying aloud of a poem one has written. In this case it may be that the author will also have responses to her or his own presentation which will contribute to further evaluation. From an audience's point of view what is *being presented* will elicit responses to induce evaluation. The 'gathering' of these responses can in turn be directed to personal literary writing — or towards another text, set or selected.

Thus the uni-directional nature of this schematic outline is not intended to determine the sequence of events operating within the aesthetic field. From my own teaching, for example, I am very well aware that the particular means I might adopt for presenting a work to my students can be the most secure way of achieving their immediate engagement to the work. The presentation works because it enables them to focus directly upon the text. It may be that by starting work immediately upon a 'gathering', made by the students out of their own experience, the use to which that is put provides the focus of attention by which the 'stimulus' (the set or selected text: poem, novel) may be engaged. In brief, we may begin the teaching at almost any point; but any point will connect with all others in pathways which track the special purpose of literature in education.

The following exploration of 'presenting' and 'responding', leading to 'evaluation', examines some of the processes involved in the model. As useful points of reference these terms will also enable us to trace some of the other connections among those activities we would seek to promote in a full literary education.

Presentation and Response: Response and Evaluation

The critical enterprise in our study of literature will involve us in knowing and judging, whether or not we turn those comprehensions into explication. We move into and through the text in order to discover the realm of potential meaning embodied in symbolic presentation. Though the text offers itself to us, we present ourselves to the text also. The meaning of the text, for each of us, is what we have made of the text in relation to ourselves, what we make of us in relation to the text and to the responses of others to the experience of the text. Meaning is a compound of these interacting forces. Such meaning is not simply a subjective response, nor need that meaning originate exclusively with the individual. There may be cooperation in the fashioning of meaning, a sharing of responses to which each individual contributes, through a subjective extension of self into the text and an objective scrutiny of the text as a fabrication of language. For there is the text as object, a construction of language whose systems of meaning can be scrutinized, its parts related to other parts through its networks of explicit and implicatory sense. But such exclusive responding, as I have argued throughout, is partial; necessarily dependent upon responses different in character, such a detached appraisal on its own will fail to take account of the full import of the literary work as an aesthetic product.

We know, as a fact of human perception, that what one sees is a factor of how one looks. First impressions may be last impressions. The completion of the aesthetic field within which literature teaching and study operates must therefore pay close attention to the matter of *presenting* any literary work. Let me illustrate briefly, stepping for a few moments into the arena of drama. I have observed a teacher present *Hamlet* to a group of students; it was an introductory presentation, and therefore intended to fulfil the purpose (in the terms in which I have set them out) of providing a means of focus so that the students might engage with the text. In fact, the teacher chose to deliver a long lecture which clearly derived from his (undergraduate?) notes culled from a conflation of E.M.W. Tillyard's *Elizabethan World Picture* and Basil Willey's *Background to Seventeenth Century Literature*. The students meekly wrote copious notes — and were bored. I was bored. I think the teacher himself was bored.

We all know examples of bad practice, and we have all given lessons of which we are not very proud. But if we have to select which lessons to give most concentrated attention to in their devising and their delivery, then there is none more vital than this introductory lesson to a text set for study. If the students are not engaged, then learning becomes a tedious and prescriptive task to which one submits only by a subjugation of personality. Instead of 'engagement' to the significant experience which literature can both afford and promote, there is substituted a compendium of knowledge to be learned. Literature as a curriculum subject becomes detached from any connection with the arts or aesthetic experience. On the occasion to which I refer there was no sense that this text was *drama*, or that it required a special kind of enactment before it achieved its identity. There was not even any real connectedness to what the play was about — that paraphrase of set text by which many teachers choose to make their introductory presentation of a text, thus destroying, to a large extent, their students' curiosity. Such a procedure is on a par with the stimulation of excited discovery which must result from the formula which one clergyman told me he adopted for the design of his sermons: 'First', he said, 'I tell them what I'm going to say, then I say it, then I tell them what I've said.' Curiosity, whether in listening to a sermon or reading literature, is in fact the urge to know, *the desire to explore so as to understand*, the very impulse by which authentic literary (and other artistic) creations are conducted.

Following the lesson on *Hamlet* I suggested to the teacher that one might begin the play with Hamlet's soliloquy 'To be or not to be...' Structurally this is the hinge of the drama; a young man of title, of intelligence, and seemingly with all the advantages of noble birth, here contemplating suicide. Two dramatic questions are thereby immediately posed: will he or won't he? (to put the matter baldly), and what brought him to this point of contemplation? Offering this starting-point to groups of students to whom the play is wholly unknown has prompted them, I have found, to want to know. There is at least now something to attend *to*, and read *for* — directed out of the questions raised by the drama of Hamlet's monologue. The first question looks to the future of the play, the second looks back to the preceding parts of the drama. This is one of the dramatic levels at which the play operates, and it gives us access to the play as a whole. Later we shall need to explore corollary issues: whether or not Hamlet is mad, for example, or just seemingly so, whether in this soliloquy he is feigning the contemplation of suicide, revolving the matter as an entirely intellectual speculation, as it were, or whether it is a profoundly felt urge to the act. There will be the related 'fall out' of considerations to be taken into account — the death of his father and the imperative, upon him, to avenge that murder by murder. To some degree these perceptions which we take of the play will be affected by historical understandings — as we connect pertinently features of the 'background' of a society and its ethical and moral bases to the play. But it must be the *play* as an artistic production that provides the criteria for these conjunctions.[2]

Presentation, in whatever adopted manner, assembles and projects, in whole or in part, the responses which we have to a given text. The form of presentation adopted will in itself enable, inhibit, encourage, or prevent the adequate offering of certain of our responses to the work. The manner in which any work is presented will suggest, if not define, the meaning derived from it through those responses to the text, which then shape our 'evaluation' of it. Though the final sense we have made of a given work will often take intellectual shape in discursive speech or writing, a presentation founded on aesthetic principles will have concentrated on the attempt to ensure that such responses draw upon the full character of the work as *art-form*. These responses, the nexus out of which evaluation proceeds, attend to the sensuous nature of the language as well as the intellectual, and are vitally involved in our imaginative reconstruction of character, incident, and occasion. We respond to the range of sensory images deployed in a text; we respond to the rhythms of language, its aural qualities, the tones of writing and written dialogue by which we animate the print symbols; we reconstitute imaginatively scene, incident, and character from what is presented to us on the printed page. Our sympathies are engaged by circumstance. Metaphor can seize us with immediacy, and we identify something in *us* — tacitly present before, but now liberated or energized through the literature, or the metaphor is remote from us, but puzzling, even worrying, and we have a sense that it *can* become meaning for us. The contiguities, the arrangements, are intuited but we cannot yet say how they connect. There is a sense of the fittingness of things, the gestalt of art. We discover that the images of literature relate to and open perception, and that its metaphors urge us to shape conception. The encounter with literature, through which we engage with ourselves and the experiences of others, is manifold also — plural in ways which have close affinities to the artistic encounter by which the work came into being in the first place.

Such responding is recreative; the work is remade in us through our active engagement with the literature. This is not at all the same as 'decoding' a text, the analytic separating of potential significations signified in the deployment of print symbols. The aesthetic response is to the *symbolization* of experience of which the text is the surrogate; the means *through* which a reader may engage with the experience fashioned out of the text by active participation in its remaking. That experience is beyond the text; it is that to which the aesthetic conception of literature teaching is directed. To stop at the text is to play with words. The symbolization of a literary work exceeds and is different from those symbols, the words, of which it is made — just as the character of an embrace is beyond the words we use to tell of it. As we move through the text to the experience (through imaginative *reconstruction*, not analytic deconstruction) we enter and possess that experience, and may dwell within it. Reading is imaginative remaking.

That refashioning will, necessarily, vary with each reader. The saturated sense of language, to recall the Vygotskyan expression, will ensure that this is so. But, if we are to make manifest these responses to the work, we must concentrate upon using or devising some means of presenting them. It is from the concentration upon our responses that we will begin to be able to make meaning of the experience we have now possessed through the reading of the work. The literature presents opportunities, if we learn to take them, by which we might come to know. That knowing is subjectively-approached but objectively-held in the work: there is reflective reciprocity here. We test against the text itself what we think, sense, intuit, or feel we have come to know. A powerful instrument to that testing will be in the manner of our presentation of these fashioned responses. Subsequently I shall go on to suggest that the search for the most apposite presentational form by which to express these responses will itself assist in their identification. But, from this consideration of the literary response and its relationship to presentation, I wish to turn to some further features and implications of matters involved in presentation itself.

Making Meaning: Reading the Text

In one limited sense, the literature is presented when it has been published; it is there on the printed page. Now we present ourselves and engage with the text. But we are not an open or blank text upon which the poem or novel can imprint itself. To the encounter we bring predispositions, attitudes, ideas — an accumulation of all that is our own world of experience and which has shaped our reality: a world of experience and its reality which the literary work may itself augment, revise, challenge. The matter, again, was summarized by T.S. Eliot:

> . . . the author may have been writing some peculiar personal experi-
> ence, which he saw quite unrelated to anything outside; yet for the
> reader the poem may become the expression of a general situation, as
> well as of some private experience of his own. The reader's inter-
> pretation may differ from the author's and be equally valid — it may
> even be better. There may be much more in a poem than the author
> was aware of. The different interpretations may all be partial

formulations of one thing; the ambiguities may be due to the fact that the poem means more, not less, than ordinary speech can communicate.[3]

I recall vividly a discussion with an Emeritus Professor of English Literature in which the matter of D.H. Lawrence's *Lady Chatterley's Lover* became the subject of talk. It was, he insisted, 'simply one of the finest works of literature we have on the English countryside'. When I tried to direct his attention to some of the other 'bits' of the novel he retorted rather testily 'Oh, I don't pay any attention to that sort of thing.'

Here, precisely, is the dilemma for the literature teacher in the presentation of literary works to students. We have to find a means of engaging the students with what we see (and through us perhaps what others have seen) in a text, whilst at the same time ensuring that the windows of opportunity we provide are large enough for the students to make their own perceptions.

The reading of literature can be a solitary exercise. The work has been published; an opportunity presents itself for us to read it. The full activity of what we call 'reading', however, requires a great deal of the reader if the text is to accomplish itself. Structuralist critics might argue that the act of such reading is in fact co-authorship; one reads in a 'writerly' way. Indeed the text, we might say, exists only at the point of its making and at the point of its remaking — which is its reading. In education we have to give due regard, therefore, as to what knowledge and expertise is required of the reader, in order that the text can be brought into existence, and how the student can be inducted into the reading of literature. We must consider how to help the student read both with and towards understanding. That is one aspect of literary presentation.

In this sense the presenting of a text is an enactment of the ways in which its reading can invoke those responses which can lead us to knowing, to meaning. The most certain way of developing this capacity is through the students' own literary writing of poems, plays, stories, and forms drawn from other genres. Through these creative activities students learn (implicitly to begin with, through the making itself) a good deal of the knowledge of how different types of literature work. Moreover, they will learn to see principles which organize the particular form required for each of their own literary writings — simply because without form there can be no coherence. The work will fall apart. This is the direct experience of literature 'from the inside', as it were. To present literature as such a creative 'making' carries with it some necessary implications.

Some Implications for the Teaching of Literature

The role of the teacher becomes in large measure that of collaborator or co-artist (in a way similar to that in which the traditions of art schools have operated, with established artists operating alongside students). The teacher activates the creative impulse and gives direction towards its many possible identities, presenting features of the formal properties of examples of genre within which and from which creating may issue. The stimulation of art-making poses immediate questions of the teacher. Very few teachers of literature or of any of the arts will be accomplished artists in their own right. But such a notion of co-working demands that all teachers will have direct and personal experience of art-making in their own fields. The implications here for the study and teaching of literature at any level are far-reaching. Those implications have been recognised in some areas of education. In some Degree syllabuses students of literature must or may devise and submit a portfolio of their own writings. Within a Literature as Expressive Art and Performance (LEAP) programme, as it operates in some Institutions of Higher Education, that unit of the degree specifically requires that the writings must also be presented. The presentational form does not end with the writing itself. The writing may be directed towards actual performance, where it can unite with other art-forms — music and dance, for example. In such an example, the poetry or prose is dramatically inter-woven — words, music, dance, all contributing to the final theatrical form. In another example, the students might work on devising, rehearsing, and producing a radio play, based on original writings of their own. Throughout the duration of the programme many genres and forms of literary writing will be explored. The exploration is active. What students learn of literature through this active participation can then give positive direction to the ways in which they address themselves to their literary studies. In this model, students learn about literature through personal art-making.

Viewed as an aesthetic enterprise the making of literary writings moves toward the related aesthetic question of how best to present, to an audience, the results of the making. The work must be made available. As in good practice in hundreds of schools, the students' literary writings are presented in displays, in school and class anthologies of writing, and may relate to other arts within the community of the school. Poems written by the students may be worked on in art lessons resulting in a poster-poem. But not all poems lend themselves to such visual incorporation. That realization in itself shows the student's reflection upon the product of her or his own making, and a recognition of something important in the nature of the original writing. The students' own poems and stories may be presented to the audience of the classroom with or without print reproduction. Poems and stories can be presented live through experiments in the form of narration, the number of voices required for dialogue, the proxemics of the presenters, gesture and movement and mime. All of those matters take literary writing onto the stage of drama.

The availability, ideally, of a community of arts within our schools and colleges would make possible even wider opportunities for reaching out from any one arts discipline into the others. A class of first-year secondary school students, for example, started from a colour print of an Hawaiian wood carving of the War God, Ku. The students' focus of attention upon the print was developed through the simple device of asking each member in a group of three or four to tell the others something he or she had noticed about the wood carving, without repeating the same observation, and going around the group so that more and more of the print was revealed, as it were. Thus the children scrutinized the print, rather than simply looked at it; they had the beginnings of a gathering of details, comments, and observations. Selecting what each found personally most interesting, the students went on to produce their own writings. One sample of that writing was this:

The War God

The war god
Which has long brown hair,
With a big mouth
And curved teeth,
Has been carved
Out of queer wood
Accidently,
With a long sharp knife.
An indian tribe will find it,
And it will lead them into war.

Laurence Hill

From such writings the students went on to design their own war gods, in painting, and continued to explore aspects of their theme through readings drawn mainly from the myths and legends of North American Indian tribes. The idea of hunt-rounds and mimes was explored in drama and through dance, chants being devised with rhythmic (mainly percussive) effects in music — the entire production ending in each group's dramatic presentation live to all the classes in their year.

Current practice in some schools and colleges promotes a wide diversity of opportunities such as these. In others there is no community of arts, no commonality of purpose, even of belief. The opportunities might be endless, creating and re-creating directed towards a full aesthetic education for our students. First, of course, there must be an institutional will to establish the organization which enables these practices to flourish. And I know first-hand how difficult and dispiriting it is to promote *any* kind of arts activity in an institution which is a cultural desert. Within this institutional context, the notion of presenting literary and other works of art raises ultimately questions about the philosophy of education itself and the place of the arts within that conception. It insists, in the words of the Gulbenkian Report, that the arts must be seen as 'disciplined forms of inquiry and expression through which to organise feelings and ideas about experience'.[4] The arts are more than that. For it is creative art-making which frequently provides the very means by which these feelings and ideas are brought into being in the first place. Just as the young students whose art-making activities I have described briefly re-contacted the mythic traditions of a culture not their own, through the re-creative activities of presentation they were enabled to develop those ideas and feelings essential to the evaluation of their experience.

It is because of this close collaboration between presenting and evaluation that there are implications for the induction of intending-teachers of literature which pertain to the fashion in which they learned to address themselves to the study of literature. Producing one's own literary writings, even without redirection to the study of other works of literature, is a valuable educational means of encountering the world of personal experience, of shaping towards one's reality, and of coming to terms with one's own sense of being. But for those who are, or are going to be, teachers of literature, the personal experience of composing literature is surely essential. Working in the medium, working through the genres, provides a working knowledge of literary forms which can be applied to other cultural examples to be engaged or 'taught'. Such working induces perceptions and intuitions of what is to be presented in the given work and how it is to be presented.

Presentational Form

The presentation of a literary work is a form of mediation. Again, one of the surest ways of developing the capacity of presenting oneself to a text and learning how to read the work resides in the encouragement of students to make their own presentations to an audience. In Higher Education there are often only two types of opportunity afforded to students of literature to present a text to an audience. One is in the seminar; the other is in the form of essay. Both concentrations of effort move directly towards evaluating, a literary-critical method of expressing discursively the meaning of the text. Both are valuable. Both methods, sensitively and properly deployed, are instruments of learning, but lop-sided if they are the only means available by which to present versions or 'readings' of the text. Given this tradition of the literary-critical method as the only experience available to them from which to draw their own teaching of literature, a good deal of the actual practice of many literature teachers simply mimes, in reduced form, the same procedures.

Such presentations leap from the reading of text to literary-critical evaluation, an intellectual exercise in the construction of meaning. There are many other possible presentational forms through which the evaluative principle can be applied.

The evaluative principle interprets, then debates. We should recall that the construction of any given presentational form for an interpretation will, to some extent, but inevitably, shape as well as re-present that interpretation. The Marshall McLuhan cliché that 'the medium is the message' begins to approach the truth only if we include that form to which the medium has been fashioned, the context of the presentation, the presenter, the audience — *all* the determinants of meaning — within the notion of medium. Certainly what remains true is that to change the presentational form is to experiment with meaning. The presentation adopted, or evolved, may be the interpretation, or the presentation may hold within it the interpretation, as, in the context of poetry, I shall suggest in the following chapter.

Thus, offering to our students the opportunities to experiment with presentational form becomes a vital means by which they can perceive their responses *through* the mechanics of the form itself. On occasion we may, as teachers, directly introduce a particular presentational form, so to enlarge the repertoire of form within which students can conduct the interpreting principles.

Experimenting with Form — an Illustration

To help groups of intending-teachers of literature to focus on these issues I have sometimes invited them to participate in the following sets of activities, which I offer here as illustrative, not innovative. The activities are based upon a commonly-used idea: that of the 'cut-up poem'.[5] The students work in threes, on the 'language units', individual words or combinations of words cut from the original poem and retyped as sets on the bits of paper they find in their group's envelope. The 'language units' are devised in such a way that each group has different sets of the original poem. Apart from the remote possibility that groups can all remake the original, this ensures that each group can make fresh versions unavailable to any other group. Though groups have come close to the original, it has never (yet!) happened that any group has actually replicated the original precisely. If a group did so, it would not detract at all from the value of the activity, as will become clear.

I shall describe the basic procedure. The initial challenge to each group is to assemble the language-units using all of the words supplied. Here is one version made in this way (See [5] for original poem):

> Twice upon a time
> There was
> A man who had
> Two faces:
> Good and bad,
> Jekyll and Hyde,
> Two faces
> Different as hot
> And cold.
> One profile
> And two faces —
> But if one were
> Cut the other
> Would bleed.

In the following version another group elected to use some of the language-units as a title:

> *Not Jekyll and Hyde*
>
> Twice upon a time there was
> A man who had two faces
> Two faces and one profile
> Two faces different
> As hot and cold
> Not good and bad

> But if one were cut,
> Would the other bleed?

As groups complete a first version they are given the options of 'having another go' to discover further unrealized potentials of the language-units. They may, if they wish, now add words of their own, and delete from the originals if they so choose. At the same time I tell them that when they have assembled the version they like the most they must prepare to present that version to the rest of us. We must, I say, be able to *hear* the poem and to *see* the poem. A copy of the preferred version is to be made upon an acetate for showing via the overhead projector — but the work must be performed. They have decisions to make: whether to say and perform the poem first, then show the print version; show, then perform; or show and perform simultaneously. Further, all three members of the group must be involved in the live presentation. These prescriptions can lead to versions which build in some of the performance criteria — the poem now taking shape is more like a prompt script than a print poem. Rehearsal time is made available in which each group improvises and works towards its presentation — experimenting with different tones of voice, single and double voices, and choral speaking. The challenge is to animate their text, and make the performance expressive.

Three versions from different groups illustrate ways in which the students worked towards their presentations — the odd appearance of the first example is better understood if one 'sees' it as a score to be spoken by responsive voices:

> Not good and bad
> Not
> Jekyll
> and
> Hyde,
> But
>
> Two faces, different
> As hot and cold.
> If one were cut
> The other would bleed.
>
> Two faces
> And
> One profile.
>
> Twice upon a time
> There was a man who had
> Two faces

Group two chose to work on a visual version to focus their live presentation through figurative suggestion:

The third example shows immediately some of its possibilities for oral presentation, with the combined possibilities of voice:

> Twice upon a time there was
> A man who had two faces
> So he saw things in all kinds of places
> Two faces! two faces! two faces!
>
> And if one were cut the other would bleed,
> One face could sleep whilst the other could read
>
> Not hot and cold not good and bad
> One face happy and one face sad.

> Different as Jekyll and different as Hyde
> One told the truth and the other one lied.
>
> Two faces but one profile
> Two faces! two faces!
> One profile . . .

In working towards their presentations some groups discover a dramatic spatial dimension — the Jekyll and Hyde 'characters', as it were, moving together. Other groups have adopted the device of two members standing back-to-back to symbolize a Janus figure (another version I have not space to include is, in fact, entitled *The Janus Face*). In brief, the presentation itself becomes *an enactment of meaning*. The groups discover potentials of the human voice beyond the print words — devices of oral narration, of dialogue, of chant, as well as features of tone, intonation, pause, pace, rhythm and stress — as they also discover elements of movement, gesture, and ritual. The presentation incorporates interpretation; the responses to the presentation identify its characteristics through the overall effect, whether amusing, threatening, surreal, and so on.

Forms of Response — Means of Interpretation

The most important purpose in outlining this sample of work has been to illustrate the ways in which one might encourage investigations into presentational form — how one might shape response and interpretation. In this instance the form moves into drama. 'Responding', 'presenting', and 'evaluating' are closely allied processes within the aesthetic field of literature. Any one activity may connect with, or be used for, other purposes. In the above case, the 'cut-up poem' activity might be employed as a means of focusing attention upon the original poem, which is then going to be examined, or it may be employed as an introduction to Stevenson's story, *The Strange Case of Dr Jekyll and Mr Hyde*. The remaking of the cut-up original might be used as a means of access to literary writings in other modes, such as the writing of diary accounts, or short stories. The interconnecting points are many and various, as suggested in the outline of the range of activities implied in the aesthetic field.

Only through a presentation of some kind can responses to the literary experience be evaluated at all. The selection of the form to be adopted is itself a critical decision. One must decide, perhaps through experimentation, the extent to which any one form is appropriate to the accommodation of a particular set of responses. It may well be, for example, that a fuller representation of one's responses to a poem can be achieved only through composing another poem. The personal effect of the first poem is arrived at through new 'making'. The new poem achieves a presentational form in its own right, while representing also an evaluative interpretation of the original. The sight of the original poem may, of course, become wholly lost to any audience which now scans the second poem. Only the composer can say that this (the new poem) is what the original poem meant personally. This is not a problem of art. It is a problem only in education where learning must be formally assessed. Yet in an educational setting where the intention is to induct students into the significant experience of literature, such products of the aesthetic enterprise should be positively welcomed. They, too, alongside the literary criticism essays, are valid and valuable means by which education through literature proceeds.

To present is to make available. We shall have responses of varying kinds to the aesthetic experience of a literary work. There will be the direct apprehension which works through the sensuousness of image and rhythm, the tonalities and inflexions of language, and the intellectual. We concentrate our attention upon our responses to a text through the presentational form which brings them into recognizeable being so that they may be evaluated.

The manner of presentation adopted or evolved is a critical enterprise in its own right; it too involves judging, as we come to understand, and knowing as we experiment with presentational form.

Notes and References

1 Dewey, J. (1985) *Art as Experience*, New York, G.P. Putnam's Sons, p. 214.
2 The active participation in the presentation/performance of Shakespeare's plays yields realizations which line-by-line 'teaching' of the text simply cannot reach. Though outside the brief of the present book I should like to recommend Gibson, R. (Ed.) (1990) *Secondary School Shakespeare: Classroom Practice*, Cambridge, Cambridge Institute of Education — one outcome of the Shakespeare and Schools Project. There are practices detailed here, including those within the context of GCE 'A' level teaching, which would provide imaginative starting-points for the study of Shakespeare in Higher Education too. Several contributions show how the 'making of meaning' may be conducted through the expressive act of presentation — students discovering the range of their responses as they engage actively in the presentational form of the drama itself, remaking the text as performance. In Chapter 8 it will be seen that I am extending the notion of poetry, and thereby its implications for presentation, into that of 'implied drama' — thus connecting poetry and drama as they relate also, in extended ways, to Shakespeare texts.
3 Eliot, T.S. (1942) 'The Music of Poetry', in Hayward, J. (Ed.) (1963) *Selected Prose*, London, Peregrine, p. 55.
4 Brinson, P. (Ed.) (1982) *The Arts in Schools*, London, Calouste Gulbenkian Foundation, p. 11.
5 It has been suggested to me that I should add some further explanatory detail here. In preparing the cut-up units I make it my practice to prepare them in BLOCK CAPITALS only, and with all punctuation marks deleted. The reason for this is very simple: I want the students to engage in a creative activity, not attempt to reassemble the units using the clues that would otherwise be available ('That must start a line because it's got a capital letter' . . . and so on). I am not challenging the students to get as close as possible to the original, and I am not conducting a lesson on syntax — though that will become a prime concern to the students as they shift the units around, as will become clear. A variety of different ways of cutting up the poem is used so that all the groups can work with words derived from the same text. But the cutting of the units means that a group can put some of its units together in ways that are not possible to the other groups. To see how this works here is the original — the first section of a very fine poem by Dannie Abse called 'Duality' (1957, *Tenants of the House*, London, Hutchinson, p. 14):

Twice upon a time
there was a man who had two faces,
two faces but one profile:
not Jekyll and Hyde, not good and bad,
and if one were cut, the other would bleed —
two faces different as hot and cold.

I open one of the envelopes and find these language-units, in the random order in which they actually tip out on my desk now:

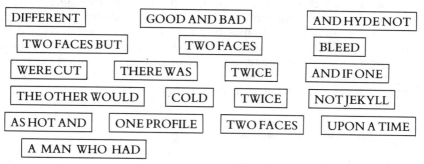

I open the next envelope and find some language-units which do not occur in the above. For example:

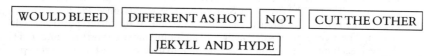

The very fact that DIFFERENT, in the first envelope, exists as an independent unit, means that it can be deployed in several combinations and still make sense. In the second case 'different' is tied to DIFFERENT AS HOT. The reverse is the case with the single unit NOT, as it appears in the first and second examples. Such differences have been deliberately built in to each collection of units, so that the contents of any one envelope do not replicate those of any other. It should go without saying that, to make any version, the students are actively and intensively engaged with language. Features of syntax and punctuation, for example, must be confronted; otherwise meaning cannot be made at all.

There is direct learning of language through knowledge of what language can do. I mention this, having had the impertinence some time ago to remind a Local Authority Adviser in English that working in and with literature, whatever else it involves, *is* language work.

Chapter 8

Sounding the Text

> Poetry is sissy stuff
> that rhymes.
>
> Nigel Molesworth[1]

'Reading' Poetry

The manner of presentation of a literary work is in itself a critical activity, and the form adopted for that presentation may itself be an expressive act of interpretation. In seeing how to present a text we have in fact already established certain key points. In the active experimentation with presenting poetry the processes of negotiating and interpreting the text have been begun; potential meaning is liberated. To develop immediate perceptual responses to a poem involves us in having a sure access to what language is and does, as, for example, in the perceptual and cognitive recognitions we make of the consequences of image, and the networks of implied meaning which the structural form of a poem sets up through a non-linear bonding of ideas. Such a remaking of meaning, in the context of poetry, demands also that due attention be given to the *sounds* of the poem, if we are to enable the student to develop a full aesthetic response — that immediate recognition of meaning in the contours of the speech of a poem. There are connections here with drama — the ways in which print symbols achieve articulation — as well as connections with other literary forms; dialogue in novel and short story, most obviously, but also with the oral narration of story.

Molesworth, in common with many students, charges at a poem ('The Brook') when called upon to recite the ill-remembered piece:

> I come from haunts of coot and hern
> I make a sudden sally
> and -er-hem-er-hem- the fern
> to bicker down a valley

Of course it is a nonsense, but a telling parody. And like all good parody, it contains a perception of truth. For whatever might have been the sense of the putative poem, in Molesworth's rendition it has been submerged in the wash of the regular accented syllable. The parody looks back to an old tradition of the teaching of poetry, in which its value was seen as an exercise in the training of memory[2] — as Molesworth's own comment reminds us:

> Even advanced english masters set THE BROOK they sa it is quaint gejeune ect but really they are all in leag with parents who can all recite it. And *do* if given half a chance.

And perhaps not just 'advanced english masters' either: I was once present at a Conference at which two HMIs tried to out-do each other's recall of passages of poetry 'learned by heart' — an odd epithet by which to describe what in most cases has been an entirely passionless exercise. Recitation is stilted, *memorized* language. It has neither the range nor flexive, adaptive character of spontaneous speech.

There is a place for recitation as performance; the tradition that belongs to the music-hall — its form is the verse monologue. It is subject to its own (usually comic), conventions, and was brought to superbly-styled realization by Stanley Holloway, among others. But it is a projection of language which clearly does not match the vocal requirements of most other forms of poetry.

On many occasions, when asked to 'Read a poem aloud', students mumble and falter; the poetry is read line-for-line, without expression, and with little attempt to make sound either match or discover sense in the print symbols. Why should this be so? The problem is seldom with the words themselves, as units of meaning, and not often with difficulties in the pronunciation of the words. Some words may be encountered for the first time, of course, but these can usually be explained quickly, or defined, or described. The vast majority of the words are already known to the students. The problem, I believe, is in two major, related, parts. They do not know how to *say* these words when encountered in the text of a poem, and they do not know how to begin to work out a way of saying them in such contexts.[3] With some students there is a tacit presumption that there must be a 'poetry-way' of saying these words, because they are in a poem. It is a misperception of what poetry is and what poetry does — in a sense that it *is* 'quaint gejeune ect.'. Consequently, there must be a 'special' way of saying aloud the words of a poem. Since they have no instruction in, or preparation for, this special production of the speaking voice, they are reluctant speakers of the words. When they do speak the words there is the barest vocal animation.

There are teachers too, at all levels of education, who will confess to their own diffidence or insecurity in the vocal projection of a poem. Indeed there are teachers who feel insecure altogether in the 'teaching' of poetry, a fact confirmed in a Report of just a few years ago,[4] and expressed by V. O'Brien in the following way:

> Asked if our preference was for teaching the novel, drama or poetry the vast majority of English teachers would opt for one of the first two.[5]

In part, such reluctance may spring from that heritage of experience by which the teachers themselves studied poetry — the making of critical ex-egeses of a poem, in an act of discrimination, which did not first engage them personally in the reconstruction of meaning. Thus, in turn, they may be uncertain as to how to make the poem a personal possession of the student, so that, in the words of a recent DES Report on poetry in schools, 'there was sparse evidence of pupils experiencing poetry in terms of personal response'.[6] Yet the formation and elicitation of the personal response is at the heart of the aesthetic enterprise in all literature, the pulse of experience against which we record those reflections from which proceed our knowing, interpreting, and judging.

That failure of the personal response, I think, may well have something to do with the miscasting of the poetic mode. I encounter regularly student-teachers (with good class degrees in English Literature) who have *studied* poetry, in seminar classes, where either there has been no aural presentation at all, or it has been fleeting — almost a brief pause before getting down to the serious business of literary critical analysis. This in turn gives us a mode of poetry teaching which presents texts as if they were some special kind of crossword puzzle to be solved. Younger students will complain 'But I don't see what this means.' Older students may conceal their ignorance but still view the poem as an exercise in sight-reading. Many teachers, however, given the task of 'teaching' the poem, will dismember and disembowel the living experience of the poem in the surgery of rhyme and half-rhyme, assonance, and the metrics of prosody. At least such technicalities can be taught with confidence, and the reading of poetry becomes an exercise in spotting the spondee. But it is a post-mortem performed on a corpse.

Treated as an exercise in sight-reading, when difficulties of comprehension arise, we are counselled to 'have another look' at the words, or some of the words, so that we can 'see' what we have been missing. In other contexts I have witnessed this dependence upon sight-reading taken to absurd extremes: the theatre-goer who takes a Shakespeare text to the production in order not to miss anything of the play; and the concert-goer with orchestrated score open upon lap in order to 'follow' the music.

Such a reliance upon visual perception is one actively fostered through the educational experience, too. Almost as soon as we learn to read aloud, as we do in the beginning, we are instructed to read silently. Good and proficient readers are those who quickly go through the part-way stage of sub-vocal reading. The good reader becomes a fast processor of information contained in the print medium; and yet there are a good many such readers who still encounter difficulties in the reading of poetry.

There are innumerable language products which are intended for sight-reading: the letter, memorandum, report, text book, newspaper editorial, and so on. In the main such reading does not demand that we put a 'sound value' to the print symbol. Most of it we read competently enough in silence. There are moments, however, in such processing of print, which provide a pertinent illustration of the argument I am advancing. These moments occur when we *do* meet with a difficulty of meaning (usually related to syntax), when we have to try out the sounds of the words in order to try to make sense of what we have already read silently. We revert, as it were, either to saying them out aloud to ourselves, or rendering them sub-vocally in our heads. Here we test out meaning by sounding the words. On such occasions we hear what we cannot see.

Poetry and Implied Drama

The sounds of language are a means to meaning. When we approach a playscript we know that the print words are to be taken as working briefs as to what is to be said and (to lesser or greater degree) how they are to be given vocalization. The actor extemporizes various ways of articulating the language of each utterance in relation to a number of contexts: the character, the nature of the occasion, what the speech is intended to serve, the relationship with other characters, the movement of the drama up to that point — these and other factors are all actively worked through in due weight and measure. I would argue that the speech of most poems is dramatic in the same sense, including those poems we might label as 'lyric' (whose examples of form in the tradition of English poetry are in any case now virtually detached from the original models).

I do not here intend that my use of drama should be taken as synonymous with 'theatre'. I take drama in the simple generic sense of 'something happening', even where the drama is internal to the conceiving, reflecting mind, and not directed to external events in the phenomenal world. There is always the implied drama of the poem itself, the presentation of otherwise wordless states of being; the drama of sensibility struggling to express itself. If nothing of this implied drama of experience, feeling, thought, or mood were happening in the poem, I would think it very hard to believe we had a poem at all. Where a poem fails to enact the drama of its own being then we are left with philosophy, rhetoric, or polemic only: on these occasions the poem fails to exceed its paraphraseable meaning.

Most poems, therefore, can be taken as speech enacting the drama of their own identity, the bringing forth of each into its being. The dimensions of that drama are predicated for us, though not necessarily explicitly stated, in that vocal projection which will realize them. To identify the character of the utterance is to explore the context of its making, which is the poem. Speech enacts its own meaning, as when someone says to you, 'Hello. And how are you today?' It might be a pleasant, offhand greeting. It will sound as such. But the gestures of the voice, the shape of the utterance, might also mean that you got a little drunk and were a little silly at the party the night before. Speech implies, as well as states. The speech of a poem, just as in ordinary speech, implies its context of utterance.

John Donne, for example, nowhere *tells* us, as readers, that 'The Flea' (1633) is a sophisticated attempt to seduce. Yet if we hear aright the tone of special pleading, by turns assertive, wheedling, obtuse, ornately argumentative, full of innuendo ('nudge-nudge, wink-wink, know what I mean?') then we begin to reconstruct the experience of the poem. Later, savouring that experience, we may, if we wish, construct or investigate that body of critical knowledge which defines the operations of the poem as a 'conceit', or that extensive body of poetry deemed somehow 'metaphysical'. But first let us witness the voice's manoeuvres as it insinuates, hesitates, pauses, challenges — and goes through the rich vocabulary of meaning that is not in words but is *of* words.

Entering the experience of a poem directly through the sensuousness of sounding the words does not require any special acting ability. Indeed there are occasions when the 'acting' of a poem attracts attention only to the performance, and away from that to which the performance should be directed. I recall hearing an actor's version of George Herbert's 'The Collar' (1633),[7] transmitted in one of BBC Radio 4's programmes, 'A Time for Verse'. The poem was presented in a rich, male, baritonal voice; the enunciation was precise. But the whole performance of the poem was conducted at the same measured pace and unaltered volume. Yet here is a man, the speaking voice, who is *angry*:

> I struck the board, and cry'd, No more.
> I will abroad.
> What? shall I ever sigh and pine? . . .

The voice of the poem is disrupted, articulation is broken — it does not proceed in regular tempo. There are breaks, silences, none of which was animated in the mellifluous flow of the performance. The performance was a failure of conception, of understanding. By working through the poem as speech one should make recognitions of the structural organization of the whole poem. For from the anger and exasperation, the heightened volume of its opening, the poem traces its variations on this crescendo to the sudden diminuendo of its close — and its quiet submission:

> But as I rav'd and grew more fierce and wilde
> At every worde,
> Methought I heard one calling, *Child*!
> And I replied, *My Lord*.

To miss these implications of the text, through its sounding, is to miss much of the experience of the poem itself — its sensuous representation of the character of the utterance.

Sight and Audition

There is, of course, some poetry which, exclusively or mainly, is 'visualist'. Such poems present a soundless vision, and should perhaps be regarded more properly as an extension of graphics. Here the point of the poem *is* in 'the look of the thing'. There is a tradition of poetry designed in such a way that its visual perception will contribute to, or comment upon, the thematic sense of the words. Layout, structure, and print innovation designate spatial dimensions within which and upon which the words themselves generate a further complicity of meaning. Since words, in their saying, have duration, then the poem is a space-time complex. Time represented by space — the gaps of layout, the space between sections, the geometry of shape. Marked examples of the last of these, each improvising its own character, exist from Herbert, through Apollinaire and cummings, to Dylan Thomas and Lawrence Ferlinghetti. To some extent every poem uses an awareness of white space as a means of orchestrating its speech. Perceived visually by the reader, and interpreted variously as silences or durations — connections and dislocations — these, too, present visual clues to the voice's articulation, the patterning of utterance. An intricately-worked example of this is employed by Eliot in the last movement of his poem 'The Journey of the Magi' (1927):

> All this was a long time ago, I remember,
> And I would do it all again, but set down
> This set down
> This: were we led all that way for
> Birth or Death? . . . .

The line-endings guide the articulation which one hears. There is hesitation, uncertainty — from the assertive 'but set down', which disappears instantly into the white space of silence and is taken up again in its repeat, to the dislocation of 'This set down' likewise hanging uncertainly as to what is to be set down — followed by a repeat of 'This' which, in the event, itself emerges only as a question tentatively framed. There are as many possible meanings to this last movement of Eliot's poem as there are possible ways of saying these words. The confusions of the speaker are dramatized directly in the ambiguities of layout, and the syntactical uncertainties created by that formal distribution of print. Layout, therefore, may also offer visual clues to audition.

The overwhelming tradition of poetry in English is founded on a form of speech-making — whether formal or informal in its mode of speech; whether intimate confession, conversation, or public rhetoric. This is so even where layout and typography follow conventional patterns or where, as in the case of the Eliot poem, the work diverges from the regularities of line-length and stanza — and in many other poems cannot be applied at all.

Poetry as Organized Speech

A poem is a form of organized speech. To approach poetry as an aural experience promotes perceptions based on our responses to the sound of the thing. It is indeed, I shall suggest, our principal means to the meaning of a poem. In this approach we shall be listening for meaning rather than looking for it. To this listening we bring a vast repertoire of tacit knowledge: of how language as speech works — its silences (protracted or as brief pauses), pace, stress, tone, intonation, loudness.

Here is a small, and fairly obvious example of what I mean by sounding the poem. Take this anonymous, fifteenth century poem:

> O westron wind when wilt thou blow
> That the small rain down can rain?
> Christ that my love were in my arms
> And I in my bed again.

Now at one level, the level at which print symbol signifies paraphraseable meaning, the poem is quite clear: 'I wish it were springtime so that I could be with my loved one again.' Yet one must attend also to what one hears in the language of the poem. And what you hear depends on how you *say* the words. An experienced reader of poetry will immediately 'hear' the tones of longing in the first two lines of the poem, and the exclamatory note of impatience in the third line. But depending on how you say those three you will 'see' the last line either as flippant, a mild sexual innuendo, or as an expression of forceful desire, of physical and mental frustration. The perception of this ambiguity, this range of implication, presents us with differing, yet simultaneously-related ways of looking at the situation. By finding ways of saying the words of the poem the reader has participated in the re-creation of potential meaning. Sounding the words here enables us to enter the richer experience of the poem — alternatives of meaning not opposed but conjoined: mental pain expressed in the form of a joke — one common way of coping with such experiences.

What I am outlining simply comes down to the suggestion that as readers we should experiment with different ways of *saying* the words of a poem. It requires no special acting skill, and will certainly not be generated out of the reverential and rather precious reading of poetry one has witnessed in many, but by no means all, Poetry Readings. What is called for is a first-order improvisation. Students, of all ages, and their teachers automatically gesture with the voice in anything they say — outside of the context of poetry. The voice naturally and fluently *comments on its own production of meaning*.

The notion of poetry as organized speech therefore provides a starting-point from which to take students into the implicatory systems of meaning set up in the words of poems, by using the characteristics of their own talk. This, at least, is something of which they have vast experience. For speaking is the mode of language as we first experience it in our development — for which reason linguisticians refer to speech as 'natural language'. We acquire facility with the written and print mode of the language later in our development — miming the secondary origin of written language as it appears in the history of cultures. In drawing upon those tacit reserves of knowledge about spoken language (subsumed within that large experience of speaking and being spoken to) we learn how to return the print of the poem to the sounds of speech, thus vivifying the words anew so that they become an *act*, and the poem becomes a speech-act. All students have such knowledge: in speaking they use freely the range of features of spoken language which express and convey thought, feeling, attitude and emotion. Hear how they talk among and between themselves — the voice animating, dramatizing the experiences which they exchange in an expressive vocal range. Then contrast the undifferentiated monotone of their 'reading aloud' of a poem in class.

The Improvisation of Meaning

One may begin the exploration into the aural qualities and suggestiveness of poetry by starting with simple 'found' sayings. Here is one:

125

'Just tell me what you think.'

As a simple mechanical exercise, just deciding where to put the major stress of the utterance will yield several realms of implied meaning. One, with the stress on 'think', can sound an invitation ('I have been waiting to find out — I would like your opinion'). Another, with the stress on 'me', invites confidential admission ('You can tell *me*'). A third possibility, stressing 'tell', might suggest exasperation on the part of the speaker. There are other possibilities too — each the resultant of a set of circumstances which we could begin to identify: saying it *this* way suggests something of the character of the event(s) which would produce this way of saying.

In small activities such as these, in practical lessons aimed at breaking down inhibitions which prevent the expressive saying of poetry, we may begin. The building of confidence can start even in this mechanical way — by moving the stress along to different words. Here is a three-word utterance. I have indicated how the stress may be shifted, and suggested in brackets the change of meaning effected by the move:

Shut that door! (. . . and that's an order)
Shut *that* door! (. . . not the other one)
Shut that *door*! (. . . you can leave the window open)

If we now start to alter intonation patterns as well, we can generate further implications of meaning, without changing any of the words themselves. If now we say

        shut

                         door

              that

we should be able to hear a different intonation pattern — the note of exasperation that says 'How many times do I have to tell you to shut that door?'[8]

And so we may proceed, taking 'found' sayings, or improvising the speech of a poem to be studied. Here, we can employ the oral resources of students, their improvisation of the sounding of the text, as a focus of attention to a whole poem. Almost any poem can lend itself to the exercise of sounding the opening line (or unit of meaning), so activating the implicatory systems of meaning generated through the discovery of differing ways of saying the lines. On other occasions we may 'snapshot' lines from the body of the text for this imaginative re-creation of potential meaning. In both cases the intention is to bring back into the *saying* of the words of a poem those animations of the voice which we would ordinarily perform in actual speech.

We might, for example, as I have done in workshop, take just two words: 'I am. . .' How many ways may these words be sounded? There is the flat statement of fact ('I am an engineer, a teacher . . .'); and there is the smug self-satisfaction of John Betjeman's poem ('I am a young executive' . . . from the first line of 'Executive', *Collected Poems*, 1974). There is also the petulant foot-stamping of the small child ('I *am*, I *am*, I *am* ...'). The words may be a scream, a defiant gesture against the odds of the universe ... and so on. By locating the sounding of these two words within possible contexts of utterance, the students actively explore a range of possibilities. We may then put these expressive possibilities back into the poem:

I am — yet what I am none cares or knows ...

Now some versions of the aural possibilities of 'I am' must be discounted, — since they must relate as precursor to the following phrase and make possible the utterance of 'yet what I am', this in turn modulating 'none cares or knows'.[9] How one will hear this opening line of John Clare's poem will significantly shape what one takes to be the experience engendered through participation with the text. In the novel form frequently this work of active listening is done for us within the text itself. I open at random the text nearest to me. I read an exchange between Gerald and Birkin in D.H. Lawrence's *Women in Love* (1920). After Birkin's berating of Gerald I read: 'Gerald sat laughing at the words and the mocking humour of the other man.' I am told, therefore, and more or less directly, how to hear the quality of Birkin's speech. Or, using the same random dipping, I open the pages of one of the most 'detached' of short story writers: James Joyce, and 'The Dead' (in *Dubliners*, 1914). I read Gretta say: 'O, I am thinking about that song, "The Lass of Aughrim".' Immediately then I read: 'She broke loose from him and ran to the bed and, throwing her arms across the bed-rail, hid her face. Gabriel stood stock-still for a moment in astonishment...' Again, though using different narrative devices, the text comments on the production of meaning of Gretta's words.

So the novel in general, by its conventions, is much more explicit than the poem in its direction to the auditory nature of speech. The novel, through its description of the way in which a character says something and through authorial or other comment, directs its effects upon the listener — whether the immediate audience of a character present in the text, or the audience of the novel. Playscripts may offer fulsome direction or none at all.

In the latter case, and with virtually the whole of poetry, we must therefore improvise the sounds of the speech — to find a way of saying which is compatible with the context and the occasion of its utterance. Each discovered way of saying the words predicates that situation or circumstance — why they are said, in that way, on that occasion. In lyric poetry, no less than in dialogues within the novel or in playscripts, we encounter the expressive qualities of the human voice, but in poetry the animation of voice resides with the auditor. To 'read' poetry we must 'say' it.

Further Improvisations

In some poems there is the opportunity, or demand, for more than one voice — traditional ballads such as 'Lord Randal' or 'Soldier, Soldier ...'; ballads by Auden ('O What is that Sound ...' 1958), or Causley ('Mary, Mary Magdelene', 1961). There are poems, such as Dannie Abse's 'The Trial'

(1957), which students may be challenged to 'score' for voices, or Henry Reed's 'Lessons of the War' (1946), which *can* be presented as two voices, though there are other possibilities of projection. The principle of sounding the text can be applied to a more complex poetic organization — from which improvisation of voice other consequences will appear. In Eliot's 'The Love Song of J. Alfred Prufrock' (1917) what is remarkable is the range of voice implied. In one sense it is the same voice which says all the words of the poem — but in a number of different guises; from the stately and portentous to the colloquial and mocking. It is a voice which is thus so busy mimicking other voices (*their* styles and conventions), that it forgets, or is unable, to speak for itself. The voice which emerges is then that of a *poseur* — the voice of a man who lacks his own central identity, and thus must express himself through the borrowed voices of others. It is the voice of an impressionist. So at the points where the central voice, the voice of Prufrock, appears as if it is about to break into its own reality with personal utterance, the voice immediately checks itself or retreats into the world of whimsy:

> I grow old... I grow old ...
> I shall wear the bottoms of my trousers rolled.

Throughout the poem there exist these moments of potential breakthrough — but they are all pretence. The pathetic truth is in the aggrandizing, through dramatic vocal gesture, of Prufrock's own pathos:

> I should have been a pair of ragged claws
> Scuttling across the floors of silent seas.

The full context of utterance, whether of spontaneous speech or the organized speech of poetry, is not determined solely by the denotation of the words used and their habitual connotations. This is to treat speech simply as an alternative form of print. Speech is personality in action — the personality projected via the poem and not necessarily the personality of the poet; the *personae* of Eliot (Prufrock, or that colloquy of voices in *The Waste Land*, 1922) and those of Browning's monologues, for example. To listen to these voices is to locate a way of saying which, both consciously and unconsciously, liberates and accumulates a range of effects, all of which substantially contribute to what we shall take to be the meaning of the poem. It is to these effects which we, as listeners, attend; and, in attending, judge. We judge, predominantly among other things, the speaker's attitude to self, to others (including ourselves as readers), and to the topic or subject of the poem. We learn, too, that speech not only reveals but conceals meaning: as when we perceive the motivation of the speaker in Browning's 'My Last Duchess' (1864) — what is not said, or only part-said, being the implicit realization of what has been said. The pauses, the fractional silences between the words render a tone whose implication provides an essential gloss on the very words being spoken.

To approach poetry as an organization of speech draws upon one's own intuitive and implicit understandings of the ways language operates through its sound patterns. Students have this understanding in their own production of speech and in their attendance upon the speech of others. Such features of speech are themselves generators of meaning (and was it not an American marriage guidance counsellor who claimed that most disruptions in relationships were caused through tone of voice?) In any act of speech we all employ, necessarily, devices of meaning which are integral to what is being said: the voice animating, replicating, and conveying attitude, emotion, mood, feeling.

Approached in this way students might bring to poetry the confidence of their everyday use of language. There will remain alternative approaches to given poems, and there will be other activities on which we focus — lingering upon image, connecting across the networks of words within the text, offering historical, scholarly and critical information as a means of sharpening the focus of attention — all these will remain. There will be, too, the vital process of mediation by which we share our perceptions through talk. But at some point there will be the sounding of the text. Through this process of sounding the text, the poem is made into an active exploration of the student's own resources; where it is a participative act, they will hear possibilities produced by others in the group. (Working in threes, to begin with, certainly helps reduce any initial embarrassment). Different versions help students explore, in an immediate way, the tricky notion of ambiguity. We may have two or more versions which provide credible readings. If we can hear them, then we may resolve them into a more inclusive understanding, which subsumes them both: different readings are not necessarily incompatible.

There is a sensuous quality to poetry. That very sensuousness — its immediate effect upon us as listeners — is a maker of meaning. In the sounding of the text we are led to *hear* what we might easily *overlook*. To promote that audition of poetry, it seems to me that we should concentrate very direct energies to the promotion of the students' own *production* of meaning. In the improvisation of that production of meaning we ask, 'How might this sound?' or 'How might this be said?' For saying a poem is, in itself, an expressive act of interpretation. The interpretation is in the performance. And in this creative engagement with poetry we might avoid turning this 'sissy stuff that rhymes' into that recitation or precious declamation which reinforces once more many students' perception of poetry as something remote from the texture of their own living.

Notes and References

1 Nigel Molesworth is the invention of Willans, G. and Searle, R. (1973) *Down With Skool*, London, Collins, Armada p/b.
2 See Schayer, D. (1972) *The Teaching of English in Schools 1900–1970*, London, Routledge and Kegan Paul.
3 The proper forum for encouraging the development of these abilities in the sounding of poetry is, of course, the classroom or workshop — and the proper medium for the exploration is that of speech itself. Some of the print examples used in the outline which follows may be found on audiotape, designed for classroom use, together with further suggestions for practical activities in an

accompanying booklet, in: Webb, E. and Lee, E. (1985) *The Sounds of Poetry*, London, Sussex Publications Ltd.

4   See Benton, P. (1986) *Pupil, Teacher, Poem*, London, Hodder and Stoughton Educational.

5   O'Brien, V. (Ed.) (1985) Preface to *Teaching Poetry in the Secondary School*, London, Edward Arnold.

6   Department of Education and Science (1987) *Teaching Poetry in the Secondary School*, HMSO 1987, p. 62.

7   Herbert's 'The Collar' and Donne's 'The Flea' will both be found in Gardner, H. (Ed.) (1957) *The Metaphysical Poets*, Harmondsworth, Penguin, p. 133 and p. 55 respectively.

8   Based on workshop activities with Edward Lee, I might mention as an aside some of the musical possibilities which can emerge out of the discovery of intonation-patterns — making for expressive possibilities across the arts of literature and music. Taking a line of poetry strictly as the 'tune', the variations in pitch of the speaking voice, students can improvise their own musical compositions. Transposed to the stave, there is already the suggestion of a musical theme — which may then be 'stretched' (to give greater pitch variation), inverted, broken into smaller musical units and rearranged, and played to different tempi. Consider, for example, the musical variations which can be promoted through the sounding of: 'Shall I compare thee to a summer's day ...'

9   'I am', in Robinson, E. and Powell, D. (Eds) (1984) *The Poetry of John Clare*, Oxford, Oxford University Press, p. 361.

Chapter 9

The Critical Enterprise: Knowing, Judging, and Evaluation

Another word for performance
is interpretation; and interpretation is another word for
reading.

Frank Kermode[1]

The Making of Personal Response

Through our responses to the literary experience we move towards evaluation. Evaluation is a judgment at which we arrive. At a personal level such
judgment puts, as precisely as we may, the effect of the literary work upon
us. It says 'what we have made' of the work based upon our responses to that
individual form. Such personal responses are founded on the interaction of
text and reader: what one takes *to* a text is in some ways as important, and
indeed in some ways predicates, what one will take *from* a text. The illustration used in the first chapter of this book, the excerpt from Melvyn Bragg's
The Maid of Buttermere (see p. 8) is meant to remind us that the encounter
with any new experience is related to the disposition of the one who is
experiencing. The episode shows us that openness to new experience is
essential, otherwise all that will be seen is what one wishes or expects to see.
The prospective reality of new experience is perceived through, and may be
destroyed by, the existence of past experience. The old reality exerts itself —
the potential for new reality given no opportunity to *be*; such judging is
prejudging, which is prejudice. Thus the episode reminds us that, for something to be seen, we need to know how to view it. In the appraisal which we
will make of a literary text, there are clearly contexts — personal and more
detached — which may influence the judgment at which we arrive.

What one brings to a text will inevitably have consequential effects upon
what one makes of the literary experience. There are, for example, contexts
of knowledge — what one has learned outside of the text now being evaluated — through which one may view the work. They may be systems of
belief, or personal attitudes. They may be issues or ideologies through which

the text is screened, which may lead to a Marxist or feminist reading of the same text. They may be bodies of knowledge, of psychology, of sociology — again part of the predisposition of the reader. Such screenings filter the work and predispose the reader's approach to the reconstruction of the experience, to which the text itself is the other coordinate, mapping out the territory of the literary experience. Some of these systems of knowledge, belief, and attitude can be positively helpful in engaging attention to the literary experience. Knowledge of conventions and traditions may illuminate areas of the text for us — to see, for instance, that the castaway's discovery of the footprint in the sands occupies structurally the mid-point of the novel, enables us to begin to recognize the design of Defoe's *Robinson Crusoe* (1719). What we had perhaps at first taken as a continuous narration, simply going from event-to-event, thereby turns out to be distinctively patterned; incidents prior to this discovery echo in incidents which follow. Such a chiastic structure then begins to challenge the reading of the novel as a demonstration of the theme of *homo economicus*[2] and, in connection with the religious background of which the novel partakes, starts to assert Crusoe as an exemplar of a spiritual condition. Crusoe becomes *homo spiritus*.[3] Scholarship devoted to establishing the conventions and conditions in which Shakespeare's dramas were first played provides insights into their organization for production — as the recent findings of archaeologists working on the newly-discovered *Rose* and *Globe* playhouse foundations in Southwark may well contribute other considerations.[4]

Scholarship, understanding of traditions, convention and genres, together with the critical interpretations of others, can all inform the eventual evaluation within which personal responses can locate themselves, and generate a larger context of understanding. But they can also presume an objectivity which may mislead, perhaps even take us away from engagement with the literary experience to which the text and our responses direct us. What is one to make, for example, of these summary judgments?

> ... Wordsworth frankly had no other inspiration than his use, as a boy, of the mountains as father-substitute, and Byron only at the end of his life, in the first cantos of *Don Juan* in particular, escaped from the incest-fixation upon his sister which was til then all he had got to say.[5]

In the teaching of literature the delicacy of balance to be achieved by the teacher rests upon the attempt to engage students with the experience to be re-created from the text, so that they fashion their own responses, whilst at the same time offering them those perspectives by which they may more certainly know how to begin that reconstruction. Fundamental to this way of proceeding is the demand that they be enabled to see the inner workings of a text, the means by which the composition coheres to direct us beyond the text to that experience posited in the writing.

Expectations: Knowledge and Coming to Know

In the teaching of literature, one of the difficulties frequently met, especially, but not exclusively, with younger students, is their expectation of what a literary text is, and more vitally still, their notions as to how the text works. It is an expectation, to summarize the matter, that the text will of itself 'mean'. 'What does *it* mean?' is the question. It is a misunderstanding of the processes by which anything comes to mean — whether it is a poem, novel, newspaper report, magazine article, film or picture. It is the same error as that which was Augustus Hope's as he stood to survey 'the jaws of Borrow-dale' waiting for 'the revelation'. Many of our students, too, await the revelation, and, failing all else, will believe whatever the teacher tells them a given work means. The students, not knowing how to read a work of literature, wait passively for someone to tell them — to make meaning *for* them.

A large measure of this difficulty, I am convinced, issues from the students' unacknowledged, but fixed, view of the literalness of things. They do not know how to think imaginatively. They 'take as read' what they have not read at all. Reality is 'The Nine O'Clock News' or 'The News at Ten' — which appears to fall from the sky like manna, and is not seen as the fabrication which it is; items selected, omitted, interpreted, packaged, presented — opinion and fact together aimed at authoritativeness. Alongside such a view of the literalness of things goes, because undeveloped, the lack of ability to handle metaphor. Lacking this transforming capacity of experience, and urged on by the educational imperative (as they see it) of the need to get things 'right', they seize with alacrity upon any fact or item which appears to have substantive value. The value, as it appears to them, is in the very literalness of the information itself. Their authority for taking it so may be no more than something which a teacher has said — even in passing. Thus, in a GCE Literature paper some years ago, one candidate wrote the following response to Wordsworth's 'Daffodils':

When Wordsworth says he 'wandered lonely as a cloud' Wordsworth was not in fact telling the truth. Because at the time Wordsworth was out walking with his sister Dorothy . . .

Such literalness, as students perceive matters, is a large part of the whole educational enterprise — the concentration upon facts, facts, and more facts . . . the 'Gradgrind' philosophy of education. It would be a serious misrepresentation of the totality of school experience to suggest that this was, in fact, the case; yet it remains the dominant impression, as students themselves see things. For much of the learning which takes place within subjects is precisely compounded of realities which are external to the learner — bodies of knowledge of things presumed to have their conceptual independence of the learner. It is further expected that all individuals following that subject should end up 'knowing' the same things. So much of school study is directed to a convergent predetermined end. For example: I recall vividly the Geography teacher who showed us colour slides he had taken of topographical features gathered from his extensive travels throughout various parts of the world. 'Here', he would say, 'is a typical hanging valley.' Next slide: 'And here is another typical hanging valley.' Third slide: 'Here you see another typical hanging valley.'. . . And so on. . . All we were intended to see was what was 'typical' — the generalizing abstraction of features by which the concept was defined. All I could see on each occasion was some-thing which was *unique*. Of course there was no reason why the two versions should not be united.

In teaching literature, and the arts generally, the focus of the endeavour is not upon 'knowledge' as a body of information and facts, but upon 'coming to know'; not knowing about, but knowing *through*. Thus, the educational experience of the literary is divergent. There are as many con-texts for potential meaning as there are readers, and through them other contexts of knowledge and belief to which reading may be conducted. On occasion, what would seem to be (to the teller) valid knowledge 'about' literature, a particular work, or its author, can occlude the passage into and through the work. Barbara Hardy, a critic whose work I very much admire, provided such an example from her own teaching of literature at university level, on an occasion when she was conducting a seminar on W.H. Auden's poem 'Lullaby':

> ... in an almost spontaneous reaction to a student who wondered 'if they were married' or perhaps kept on saying 'she', I said that it was almost certainly a poem about homosexual love. I got a very violent reaction from one student, who angrily said I had spoilt the poem for him and that he wished very much I hadn't told him.[6]

I can recall clearly my own response on reading this. For years, but in ignorance of Auden's personal sexual orientation, I had had a great fondness (which I retain) for this poem; a poem I had taken as an expression of certain moods of love, without consciously thinking at all about the permutation of the sexual coupling. I went back to the poem, as I have done on many occasions subsequently and do so again now, to search for the textual clues which would enforce Barbara Hardy's assertion. I find neither a 'he' nor a 'she' anywhere in the poem; neither of the words exists in the text. There is a 'you' and there is an 'I' (and the sole 'her' of the poem is clearly tied to Venus, goddess of love).

Metaphor and Meaning

What the critic-teacher or scholar knows about an author may or may not be relevant to any item of literature produced by that author. That is one point. Another is that such an autobiographical approach to the reading of a given work can overlook the nature of the literature itself as a means of embodying experience, of referencing a context, no longer exclusively autobiographical, but one shaped towards the making of meaning rather than the record of event. The poem supplies its own context — and may distil a reflective, or projected, view rather than a confessional one. The exercise of imagination enables us to reach out from the personal, in acts of creative composition, to the metaphor. The poem, the novel, are symbolic projections, made from experience certainly, but from the whole of experience, including that which may be known other than through the actuality of lived circumstance. They are, first, acts of imagination. Through such acts of imagination the artist can reach beyond the personal.

The reader, too, approaches the work imaginatively, as metaphor. To fail to do so is to fail to get beyond the literalness of the text. It is the error made by a television interviewer who questioned A.D. Hope, some of whose writings contain images derived from sexual activity, as to why he was so obsessed about sex — as so many of his poems were obviously about that. Hope replied: 'I thought they were concerned with love.'[7]

A consideration of literature as metaphor, that symbolization of language which constructs the experience *beyond* the text, necessarily runs counter to a view of reality as prescriptive and literal. To attempt to treat literature as such poses some related challenges in its teaching. It raises, for example, the question of ambiguity: the extent to which more than one 'reading' of a text can have simultaneous validity. Those students who want to know what *it* (the text) means, want to know this as a singularity — as a definitive: 'X means Y'. Of course, this by-passes the very operations by which anything comes to 'mean'. The product of a work of art, recalling the words of John Dewey (in the epigraph to Chapter 7), is the aesthetic experience of order, through cooperation with the work, which is also *liberating*. 'Meaning', in a literary work, is also a collaborative remaking, through one's own activities — the giving and taking of reader and text. F.R. Leavis captured the point precisely:

> ... you cannot point to the poem; it is only 'there' in the recreative response of individual minds to the black marks on the page.[8]

In the educational context there is, additionally, the giving and taking of self to and from others, as we, students and teachers, exchange our recreative responses through the text. This suggests that in the teaching of literature we must devise means by which students can engage with the text and connect with others in that reconstruction of experience, directed from and by the text, which will promote the identification of meaning. To connect personally with a poem often demands that we find a means by which the students can themselves understand how the language, the symbols of the poem, conspire towards meaning — but only if we can perceive how the language of imagination works, thus what nature of activity we must bring to the reconstruction of the experience of the poem.

Words may be saturated with sense; they are ambiguous and denote and connote a variety of referents. One of the labours of an artist is to *exclude* words for this very reason — they lack the precision by which, at the least, to circumscribe the range of options to which they might be applied. Hence, to take a one-word example, Yeats's decision to change the first word of 'Sailing to Byzantium' from 'Here' to 'That', and in so doing to change utterly the arc of meaning within which one must seek actively to reconstruct the experience to which the poem directs us. Such decisions can be based only upon an extensive knowledge and understanding of what words can do. But the difficulty with many students of literature is quite the reverse: they must open their perceptions to the diversities of meaning to which words lend themselves. The words of most poems will not connect with each other if one presumes that each has a single point of contact, as it were, and the 'hook' of *the* meaning of this word will not fit into the 'eye' of *the* meaning of that word. Poetic and imaginative meaning is not constructed on the same principles as Lego bricks, made to fit with each other. They exert, rather, a kind of gravitational pull on each other according to the field of forces by which they act upon and react to each other. One feature of this gravitational pull can be called 'association'. There are others — pulled together through syntax and rhythm, for example, but association certainly is important. One can demonstrate this very simply, though I shall not record all the teaching of which this is a part.

I ask the students to begin by noting their immediate response to each word I am about to offer — not to think about it, since I am going to give the words fairly rapidly. Responses are gathered and displayed under each 'trigger' word. As an example, these words, from among those I collect from the class, are written up on a board beneath their prompts:

night	*crimson*	*secret*	*destroy*	*howling*
dark	red	lie	kill	wolves
fear	blood	guilty	end	fear
threat	rose	fear	death	night
dream	blush	shame	poison	storm

The actual list is more extensive than this, but this edited sample will illustrate how the associations of certain words are already beginning to connect with each other. Below is the full list of 'trigger' words, as previously prepared on the reverse of the board and now shown to the students:

rose

        worm

            night

    howling

          bed

crimson

      secret

     destroy

Readers of this book will clearly see in the 'trigger' words, Blake's poem, 'The Sick Rose'.[9] The point is that through a network of associations, some kind of 'image' of the poem begins to develop, in the way in which an image begins to appear on exposed photographic paper when immersed in the developer solution tray. These, from among the key words of the poem, are now held inferentially within a context as yet undisclosed. But a network of implicatory meanings, or attachments of meaning, has begun its work, by liberating such words to the functions of the imagination, and to personal memory which will feed the imagination. Subsequently one goes on to fill in the gaps so that all of the words of 'The Sick Rose' are now revealed — the associations attached to 'rose', 'bed' and 'worm' having also contributed effectively to the network. In terms of formal criticism this moves us to a stage where we can identify that the poem is 'about' love destroying, in some unspecified way or ways, the object of its love. It is a beginning, that is all, from which we can move on to a more thoroughgoing exegesis.

I have outlined this approach, used with adult students, to try to illustrate some general matters — not to commend the method in any sense for application. It is used to show that there are ways, derived from each individual work of literature, which can suggest to students some of the ways in which the language of the piece has been employed — particularly to try to break down the notion of the sequentiality of language in poetry. Poetry (and prose and dialogue within their formats) uses words to connect across and among its units. Words and their implications are not confined to the given location in which they appear in print. The meaning and resonance of any word can activate words elsewhere. Freeing students from the tyranny of literalness and conveying to them something of the interplay of words is essential, if they are to be helped to understand something of the 'mechanics' of language deployed imaginatively. It comes down to helping students to see *how* the literature works as art-form, because they have been actively engaged in the reconstruction of the poem. They have, in whatever limited manner in the early stages, at least made some kind of contribution to the poem. Without the contribution of *their* responses the poem cannot mean anything itself. A poem, or any art work cannot *impose* its meaning upon us, by and of its own volition. Provoked by our responses to the work we invoke meaning.

Representations of Experience: the Personal and Impersonal

Connected with an implicit acceptance of the literalness of literature, and the consequent difficulties of trading in ambiguity, there is another matter which can stand in the way of arriving at evaluation through the interpretation of one's own responses, one which can be so pervasive that it blocks approaches to the text as art. It is in the presumption that the work, poem or novel, is the author's own experience — that it is about her or him. It is an extension of the subjectivist view of what literary forms attempt to do, and is a heritage, in large part, of the way in which the Romantic movement in literature has come to be seen. Such a view sees the work as an expression of the person uniquely, her or his actual experience — which is to subvert all literary forms to pseudo-autobiography. But the world of experience from which literary 'making' proceeds is far more extensive than that. One may, for example, be arrested by the thought of an idea, the implications of which can be investigated only through their working out in a fictional context. One can write, and attempt to give credibility to, thoughts and impressions one would personally disown. The subjectivism is in the creative engagement with that idea, to sense and feel its import from the inside so that it may achieve representative form. The idea exists — and probably pre-exists — the novelist's preoccupation with it as a fact of existence. The literature examines the dimensions and forces of that idea as a function of personality, its reality for that character who has been figmented from the author's encounters with all that constitutes her or his personal world. This is imaginative presentation, not personal confession. The idea is put into a human context, not examined as an abstract summary or generalization. In its literary embodiment the idea is reintegrated with character where it re-connects with the psychology and motivation and living from which, as conception, it originated.

The extrapolation of those ideas, which have been creatively assembled in the work, need not necessarily correspond with those ideas the artist would claim personally. This conflation of the status of the art with the status of the artist can be particularly acute in poetry. For there the accusations might begin. A.D. Hope again supplies an apposite comment. In reply to some of the critical accusations levied against him, he replied:

> What the poem says is apt to be taken by general readers and professional critics alike for what the poet thinks or feels. In other forms of literature, in drama and fiction for example, readers have learned to distinguish the author's own attitude from opinions and ideas expressed through the characters or even put forward as part of the dramatic setting.[10]

The problem is, in fact, far more widespread than Hope believed. His optimism that readers have learned to make such a separation of views between author and work in the case of the novel, is certainly not borne out in the experience of Graham Greene — as this sample of wry humour illustrates:

> A word about the characters in *The Comedians*. I am unlikely to bring an action for libel against myself with any success, yet I want to make it clear that the narrator of this tale, though his name is Brown, is not Greene. Many readers assume — I know it from experience — that an 'I' is always the author. So in my time I have been considered the murderer of a friend, the jealous lover of a civil servant's wife, and an obsessive player at roulette. I don't wish to add to my chameleon-nature the characteristics belonging to the cuckolder of a South American diplomat, a possibly illegitimate birth and an education by the Jesuits ...[11]

The collective notice served by Barbara Hardy, A.D. Hope, and Graham Greene should serve to remind us of some of the dangers in too heavy a dependence upon autobiographical records in our attempts to engage the student with that literary experience which issues from the text. There are works which are imaginative realizations of actual lived experience, or are founded closely upon that. And there are within the corpus of literature many works whose realizations are derived not from personal biography but from personal engagement with the worlds of others, actual or synthesized — an extension of one's self into the realities of others, real or imagined. At the very least the recognition of what Eliot argued to be the impersonality of art should make us hesitate before wheeling in the standard lecture on 'The Life of the Author'.

Responses to Literature

In the teaching of literature we try to give first priority to enabling the students to derive their own responses, by making the means available to approach the text, so that they can have these responses in the first place. From this active contemplation they can move towards evaluation. In one sense and with some texts, this could mean ensuring there is sufficient unobstructed passageway for the student to approach the text directly. But as a corollary it frequently means in practice that we must devise practices by which students can make that approach — offering what I have called a 'focus of attention', to ensure that the effects of the literature can be seen. Such activities 'frame' the work, or parts of the work, so that it might be perceived in its working operations. Somehow we initiate them into the activities of all that is subsumed under the description 'the reading of literature'. At a simple level, but profound in its implications, this could be merely an exploration of a poetry text to show how the internal organization and correspondences of the text operate in an associative network, not through dictionary definitives. We should explore the dimensions of sound, in speech, so that our responses to poetry can include the auditory experience. I am grateful to one of my schoolteachers who, though he introduced the poem dismissively as an example of 'modern poetry', read aloud to the class 'Mr Eliot's Sunday Morning Service'.[12] At the phrase 'clutching piaculative pence', the potential of language as physical experience came alive for me. *Here* was a physicality of language — the saying of the words demanding energies of the speaker, forcing the mouth, throat and lips to do things. Though I did not understand the phrase, somehow there was a sense that, whatever it meant, it had something to do with these facts of its utterance; somehow it was a comment, on that part of the poem, in its own right. The cadences of Arnold's poetry and Tennyson's had not registered with me with this directness — though later I was able to hear their special sound-shapes. In dialogue, in the novel, we need to be able in like fashion to re-create the inflexions of language; the subtleties of intonation, pause, pitch, stress — the whole auditory manufacture of meaning. Irony, for example, is what you *hear* in the vocal realization of print symbols, which may not *look* ironic at all. (This in itself explains how many students fail 'to *see* the point' of Jane Austen's narratives). In novels and poetry we need to dwell within the images they employ, the descriptions they supply, connecting them back to sensory experience. All of this and much more is implicated in the endeavour to enable the literary experience to operate aesthetically upon us.

To these elements of literature we respond with directness. They are immediate perceptual responses by which we apprehend the nature of the work. Such responses tell us how the work *affects* us. Through this affective domain we come to know significant experiential matters to which the symbolization of the work directs us. Through these and other recognitions of the text we assemble matter for reflection — for interpretation and evaluation. From knowing how the work affects us we proceed to an attempt to formulate what we have now made of it. We appraise the reality of what that text means — to which judgment we may apply other contexts of understanding and knowledge. From personal evaluation we move to more detached contemplation — relating and re-cognizing, selecting and arranging within the world of personal and shared experience as we share the text — how it has affected us and what we have made of it.

In an article originally published over fifty years ago, D.W. Harding[13] proposed that the psychology of the reading of a literary text involved the reader in four modes of activity, four sets of responses. I shall use them here as terms of reference, though without binding myself to the detail (nor indeed the order) in which he presents them — using and supplementing them to redirect attention to matters I have so far tried to pose.

There is, Harding maintained, an Operative Response — 'actually doing things'. There is the act of reading itself, in which I would include those re-creative activities of, for example, sounding the words of a text. Within an educational context I would include here also those teaching devices in which the students actually do things before, during, and after their engagement with the text. There is the Perceptual Response — the enjoyment of experience at the perceptual level, or refinements of the perceptual experience. Here, for example, the reader may dwell within the visual image contained in a text; again the teacher may promote activities, the students actually doing things, which enable them to form the perception so that they may enjoy, and then go on to contemplate, that experience. There is the Comprehending Response — 'getting to understand things' as Harding expresses it, or 'coming to know' in the phrase I have adopted. Then there is the Evaluative Response — the making of value judgments, the attitudes formed from observation. Harding's exposition suggests that evaluation functions in a detached way through one's role as an onlooker of events; and that both the Perceptual and Comprehending Responses are forms of 'looking on'. I hesitate over this formulation, because even though one is looking on, literature being vicarious experience, I think there are occasions when one is looking *out* of the literary experience. There is an involvement which directs the *personal* response, of perception or comprehension — a response which will almost certainly undergo change, as one moves out of the experience and adopts a more distant, or detached perspective through reflection. This is the view from a critical stance, certainly, but it may be after the event of our involvement or participation with the text. That personal response will still be vital to the forming of the detached 'onlooker' appraisal which will end in value-judgements. Though onlookers we are at this phase *involved* in our looking on — later detaching ourselves. I think something of this order is implicated in Harding's own comment:

> In the representational arts, most obviously in literature, the author invites his audience to share in an exploration, an extension and refinement, of his and their common interests; and as a corollary, to refine or modify their value judgements.[14]

The movement is from participation (the shared exploration) to reflective evaluation. In that progress there must be something itself of value in detached evaluation, which Harding typifies as being 'more widely comprehensive':

> One views the event in a more distant perspective and relates it to a more *extensive system of information, beliefs* and *values.* And this detached evaluative response undoubtedly possesses the utmost importance in *building up, confirming* and *modifying* all but the very simplest of our values. It is as onlookers from a distance that we can most readily endure the penetration of general principles among our sentiments.[15]

Text and Context

We may attempt to summarize this movement towards evaluation in the following way, locating the text within the context of other knowledge and experience from which we begin our reading:

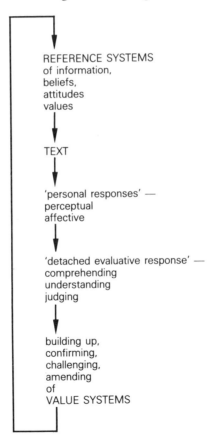

REFERENCE SYSTEMS
of information,
beliefs,
attitudes
values

TEXT

'personal responses' —
perceptual
affective

'detached evaluative response' —
comprehending
understanding
judging

building up,
confirming,
challenging,
amending
of
VALUE SYSTEMS

Of course the literary experience is not as programmatic as that, either in our readings of the work of others or in the making of our own literary writings. In the prime making of literary writing the work itself may be, at a fundamental level, the maker's response, interpretation and evaluation all in one, the work itself. The very impulse to the making of the work springs from the recognition, in varying degrees, of the fact that in this, and no other way, could we attempt to come to terms with experience, and through the presentational form of the piece hope to symbolize the nature of the experience of which it is compounded. The work presents directly what we have come to know, and may well provide the tacit sense we have made of that knowing. On many occasions, however, after the event of the writing itself, one can then (with the surprise of discovery) say: 'Now I can see what I was trying to say.' Evaluation, however imperfectly translatable into any other mode or form of realization, represents what we can say about what we have made of the full meaning of the work. Beyond the words we have used to make our evaluation, there remains a persistent recognition that only in the form of the work itself can its full stretch of sense be expressed. Beyond 'the detached evaluative response' of our making, we return to the art, the literary writing. Ultimately, there is no other way in which Shakespeare's 'multitudinous seas incarnadine' can be said.

Expressive Evaluation

I have suggested earlier that there are limitations to the discursive form of the literary-critical essay to which much of our students' writing is directed. It is the presentational form which characterizes the tradition of literature teaching as it has come down to us today, and the common form for the evaluation of a literary work. I have also said that it is, or rather can be, an invaluable means towards the development of learning. But an education *through* literature must aim to develop other possible presentational forms within which students can arrive at their responses, and the responses of others, to any given text. The recent introduction of GCSE English and GCSE English Literature has given a great momentum to such developments by bringing together (in some syllabuses) suggestions deriving from some of the best current practices. Overlooking any demerits of the system of GCSE and its ponderous mechanisms, there is, within the practice of GCSE teaching, much which addresses itself directly to the point of literature as an arts conception.

To begin with, the English syllabuses now insist that some part of the delivery of the programme must concentrate itself upon literary texts. This is in addition to the separate English Literature syllabuses. Given the drift of English away from any necessary engagement with literature over the past decades,[16] this is in itself a welcome declaration. What is also to be welcomed is the recognition that expressive and imaginative presentations are both allowed and to be encouraged. The essay remains, quite properly, but a thoroughgoing exploration of literature at any level, including degree studies, might well attend to alternative forms of expressive and re-creative writing as a means of moving towards evaluation. Such writings would promote active engagement with a variety of literary forms, not only to promote the students' own creative writings, but also as ways of engaging with the texts to be studied. Among the suggestions for assignments contained within one English Literature syllabus (Southern Examining Group, Syllabus B), for example, we find the following — which might equally be employed within the English programme:

- consideration of the means by which literary texts may be transmitted: e.g. mass media, poetry readings . . .
- diaries kept by characters
- imagined encounter between characters from different texts
- reconstruction from the perspective of a minor character
- a chapter or scene which might be inferred from a text
- script for a radio programme of poems on a theme

Activities such as these[17] collectively serve a number of purposes. To take the first and last examples together, these clearly focus on presentation (rather than the 'transmission' of the first example, as written) — thus the need to concentrate on matters of audience as well as presentational form. Creating the link material between the poems, both as introductions and as commentary, engages the student with the poems themselves, so that the whole movement of the literary experience from reading to personal response and evaluation must be followed through before *and in the making* of the programme. The expressive qualities of poetry as sound must be investigated, the text animated through the voices of the speakers who are to say the poems, so that improvisation and experimentation with the effects of that oral realization also become important activities.

Other creative potentials of expressive writing can lead the student into an understanding of the conventions and practices of distinct literary genres. Encounters between characters from different texts (or from the same text, but in a setting not employed in the novel itself) compel us to attend to what we have come to know of character through the improvisation of their responses to each other. The presentational form may emerge into playscript, dialogue and description in novelistic form or impressionistic description. Seeing things through the perspectives of minor characters (Rosencrantz and Guildenstern) forces us to have another look at the text.

Some writing can issue very simply out of the motivating of curiosity. Here, for instance, are the beginnings of three different writings all prompted by lingering within the possibilities inherent with the very first sentence of a short story ('The Baron', 1911) by Katherine Mansfield:

(1)   'Who is he?' I said. 'And why does he sit always alone with his back to us, too?'
    'I don't know, dear. Do be quiet, there's a good boy.'
    'Doesn't he like us, then?' I asked. 'He never says "Hello", he just keeps round that way, back to front all the time.'
    'Oh, I expect he's happy that way. Yes, I'm sure he's happy.'

'I expect he's very old and it's hard for him to move about. He's very quiet.'

'Well, yes, and perhaps you should be quiet too. It'll be our turn soon and you'll have plenty of time to talk then, won't you?' She was getting cross, I could tell ...

(2)   Who is he? Why does he sit always alone and with his back to us too?

His overcoat collar turned up, close to his ears, the shoulders of the coat still glistening from the rain; his greying hair, dark with wetness, clinging to his skull, not smoothly but with a damp profusion of wispiness.

His hands, large, veined, veined, sinewy, curled around the white chipped mug ...

(3)   'Who is he?' I said, 'and why does he sit always alone with his back to us too?'

The company looked at me. I felt embarrassed, I obviously shouldn't have asked. Derek nudged me and mouthed 'I'll tell you later'. The talking went on and I looked around me. The room was large and high like a cathedral. At one end of the room was a large fireplace with a blue Dutch tile surround and the meanest of fires burning in the grate. I shivered and drew my cardigan around me. Still the interminable talking ...

Just as these students' curiosities were aroused by a contemplation, within their own imaginative syntheses of experience, of the first sentence of Katherine Mansfield's story, readers of these excerpts may well be curious in their turn to know how each writing went on from the point at which it was cut. At the least, it is clearly evident that here are three very different treatments — each of which demonstrates the use of various narrative and descriptive techniques. I cite them here, however, merely to show that the impulse to create out of the initial stimulus connected also with an engagement to the Mansfield text. Having made *their* explorations, the students wished to know what the original writer of the first sentence had done with that opening (since they did not know, until the completion of their own writing, that the writer was Mansfield). Approaches, such as this, illustrate how the making of literary writing can be used to introduce a set text; the students' making of personal writings interacting with their reading of other works. Within a conception of literature as art the aesthetic field of activities connects in all directions among making, re-making, presenting, responding, and evaluating — and suggests three principal types of activity to be promoted. In a creative approach to the teaching of literature one would seek to promote activities aimed at:

- connecting the student *to* a text
- enabling the student to explore *within* a text
- and encouraging reflections leading *from* a text

Any one of these functional categories might take the form of expressive writing, though there is a wide variety of other activities which might be used to supplement writing: role-play, discussion, activities such as the cut-up poem, word and image association, and so on. We might go from a snippet of text to personal writing; from personal writing to set text. In and through these activities we shuttle between making and remaking, creating and re-creating meaning. In and through all of these expressive activities we promote the literary-critical response that ends in evaluation. But we have made the experience personal; the literature is now a part of our personal worlds of experience. For evaluation is not simply something that you do *to* or *upon* a work of literature. One works *with* a text. In appraising our responses we realize something of ourselves. Both in the adventure into personal literary writing, and in the collaborative venture of exploring the literary experience, we found our realities and learn to evaluate them.

Notes and References

1 Kermode, F. (1975) *How We Read Novels*, Southampton, University of Southampton, p. 17. I should make it clear that Kermode is here commenting upon the proposition of Umberto Eco that 'every work of art . . . is effectively open to a virtually unlimited range of possible readings, each of which causes the work to acquire new vitality in terms of one particular taste, or perspective, or personal performance.'
2 The classic reading of Crusoe as 'an embodiment of economic individualism' will be found in Watt, I. (1957) *The Rise of the Novel*, London, Chatto and Windus.
3 For a detailed exposition of the chiastic structure of *Robinson Crusoe* and its relation to a spiritual reading of the text see Brooks, D. (1973) *Number and Pattern in the Eighteenth Century Novel*, London, Routledge and Kegan Paul, pp. 18–26.
4 A general account, with illustrations and photographs, of some of these findings can be found in Webb, E. (1990) *Literary London: an Illustrated Guide*, Tunbridge Wells, Spellmount. Fuller and more technical details may be found in Hildy, F.J. (1991) *New Issues in the Reconstruction of Shakespeare's Theatre*, New York, Peter Lang.
5 Empson, W. (1956) *Seven Types of Ambiguity*, 3rd. edn., London, Chatto and Windus, p. 20. In the same passage summary judgments are passed also on Keats, Shelley, Browning, Meredith, and Coleridge.
6 Hardy, B. (1973) 'Teaching Literature in the University', *English in Education*, 7, no. 1, p. 30. Negotiating such responses can, of course, lead to an even more intense scrutiny of the responses of self and others to the text — given sensitive teaching and the belief that such explorations are indeed the purposes which inform the study of literature. I should like to direct the reader to those observations which Barbara Hardy herself made of the incident she refers to: 'The strong and unexpected response took me into further reflections about the nature of the poem, and eventually to further reflections about homosexual and heterosexual love-poetry, homosexual and heterosexual love. The teacher's tolerant, liberal, bland voice, the student's intolerant, candid, angry voice and the poet's veiled, troubled, masterly voice joined in a unique occasion. Untied, the thread led off in different directions. The occasion was alive. Poem, student, teacher, were all changed.' Here, precisely, is the interactive coming to know, *through* the text (the 'third voice' in the classroom), in ways which are both personal and social — because they are shared.

7 Hope, A.D. (1965) 'The Sincerity of Poetry', in *The Cave and the Spring*, Adelaide, Rigby, p. 68.
8 Leavis, F.R. (1962) *Two Cultures?*, London, Chatto and Windus, p. 28.
9 The full version of Blake's poem is as follows:

The Sick Rose

O rose, thou art sick!
The invisible worm
That flies in the night,
In the howling storm,

Has found out thy bed
Of crimson joy,
And his dark secret love
Doth thy life destroy.

Much anthologized, the poem will be found, for example, in Hayward, J. (1956) *The Penguin Book of English Verse*, Harmondsworth, Penguin, p. 241.
10 Hope, A.D. *op. cit.*, p. 70.
11 From the Dedication of *The Comedians* (1966) London, The Bodley Head. Greene, in the same place, also reminds us of the nature of imaginative experience: ' "I" is not the only imaginary character: none of the others ... has ever existed. A physical trait here, a habit of speech, an anecdote — they are boiled up in the kitchen of the unconscious and emerge unrecognizable even to the cook in most cases.'
12 Eliot, T.S. (1969) *The Complete Poems and Plays of T.S. Eliot*, London, Faber and Faber, p. 54.
13 'The Role of the Onlooker' (1937) in *Scrutiny*, Cambridge, Deighton Bell, VI, 3, pp. 247–58.
14 *Ibid.*, p. 258.
15 *Ibid.*, p. 252. Further reflections on the evaluative process will be found in Harding, D.W. (1962) 'Psychological Processes in the Reading of Fiction', *British Journal of Aesthetics*, II, 2, pp. 133–47.
16 A movement I have traced briefly in 'The Case of English: English as Aesthetic Initiative', in Abbs, P. (Ed.), *Living Powers: The Arts in Education*, London, Falmer Press. I must add here that some of the recent advances made possible through GCSE English and English Literature are currently under threat. Their introduction made possible a 'dual-certification' in secondary schools — a unified course which enabled students to gain both English and English Literature qualifications in GCSE. In many schools this enabled teachers to 'lead' the programme through work arising directly from literature in such a way that the criteria for both GCSEs were met. In this scheme of things students are exposed to a significantly wider experience of literature. With the introduction of the National Curriculum and a compulsory minimum time to be allocated exclusively to the GCSE English programme, the pressure upon the secondary timetable will almost certainly mean that many students will read far less literature than is the case at the moment. Their experience of literature will be limited to the small proportion required for GCSE English. GCSE English Literature is likely to become an optional course of study, where it survives. There is another restraint. From 1994 the revised regulations for GCSE English and GCSE English Literature will prevent schools offering to their pupils courses assessed by 100 per cent coursework. From that date 30 per cent (minimum) of the total assessment must be accounted for in a formal, terminal examination. Inevitably, some of the im-

aginative and innovative teaching which 100 per cent coursework made possible will be curtailed, as teachers and their students concentrate upon 'the exam'. Though 'only' 30 per cent of the total assessment, that amount will loom much larger in the minds of the students.

17 Such approaches ('active strategies' as there called) are endorsed in the Department of Education and Science (1989) *National Curriculum Proposals for English for Ages 5 to 16* (The Cox Report), HMSO. See, for example, paras. 7.8–7.10.

Afterword: Sensibility and Sense

> Our response to literature is affective
> and personal, and so should be capable of
> changing not only in relation to the other
> readers to whom we talk about literature
> but also in relation to our own growing
> and living.
>
> Barbara Hardy[1]

The central argument of this book has been that literature in education must be approached as art. As art literature does not constitute a *body of knowledge*, but rather a *means* by which one may come *to know*. Literature is always meaning in this personal mode, whatever the conventions and the structures of any individual work. These may, for example, adopt the device in narrative of the distant, removed observer and commentator on other people's actions, thoughts and beliefs. But the narrative is formed so as to enter that world of experience, to engage creatively with that world of experience so that its reality may be known. That reality is the shaping of the work itself; it can not be known in any other way. For in literature (as in other arts) there is a subjective extension of self into the object of one's regard, one's contemplation. In that extension potentially the whole of one's personal world of experience provides the resource out of which engagement with the 'making' proceeds. And it is precisely here, in its composition of experience, that literature affects us — where extrapolated facts and data and knowledge fail to excite us; because in literature we encounter the sense of *living experience*.

It is essential that students be given the opportunity and the encouragement to construct, in literary forms, the realities of their own experience. Through their own writings they will move towards self-realization; they will come to know and to understand themselves, and themselves in relation to others. To that end students will need to be presented with a wide range of the literary forms and modes of different *genres*, the exploration of whose characteristics enables students to extemporize and experiment towards a shape of writing which will most fittingly realize individual versions of reality.

The prime making of the students' own literary writings will thus be one of the most important features of any literature programme founded on aesthetic principles. Such personal writing, however, is itself intimately connected with the study of literature. It may lead into the study of a text, explore features and aspects within the text, and may arise from that study. There will be a shuttling to and fro between the making and the 'reading' of literary writings.

Reading itself will acquire a wider concept of practice. Students will be inducted into the means of enjoyment of the perceptual and aesthetic dimensions of literary forms so that they may respond with direct sensuous apprehension to the text. That appraisal will itself importantly illuminate perceptions of meaning and contribute to comprehension. For literary forms invite us to dwell within such sensory and affective modes of apprehension, our responses significantly shaping what we shall make of the text. Reading itself is the means by which the reader first activates the text, then, in cooperative inter-action, creates a version of that experience symbolized by the text. Such interpretations may be conducted through a variety of activities — themselves expressive acts which may begin with the talking *out* and *through* of experience. Other activities may take us into an active exploration of varying presentational modes by which to realize more fully the nature of that experience. Additionally, reading may be realized through performance — as in the active experimentation with the sounds of a poem. The notions of creative transposition enable students to explore further the aesthetic field of literature. Within that field, reading, response, interpretation, comprehension, presentation, performance, and evaluation are all significant points of reference. These are the terms which identify the nexus of opportunities for the teaching of literature as an aesthetic enterprise.

Their exploration is the imaginative journey which literature proposes into one's own world of experience and the worlds of experience of others. Within the creative possibilities of these terms resides the potency of the *art* of literature as a symbolization of experience, through which we come to know ourselves and others personally. For literature, as all the arts, vivifies our sense of being, and through that enrichment of our sensibilities, enables us to begin to make sense of the world of our realities.

Reference

1   Hardy, B. (1973) 'Teaching Literature in the University', *English in Education*, **7**, 1.

Select Bibliography

On Symbolization, Creativity, and the Arts

ABBS, P. (Ed.) (1987) *Living Powers: The Arts in Education*, London, Falmer Press.

ABBS, P. (1989) *A is for Aesthetic: Essays on Creative and Aesthetic Education*, London, Falmer Press.

ABBS, P. (Ed.) (1989) *The Symbolic Order: A Contemporary Reader on the Arts Debate*, London, Falmer Press.

ARNOLD, M.B. (1961) *Emotion and Personality*, 2 vols., London, Cassell.

ARNOLD, M.B. (1968) *The Nature of Emotion*, Harmondsworth, Penguin.

BEST, D. (1985) *Feeling and Reason in the Arts*, London, Allen and Unwin.

BRUNER, J.S. (1967) *Towards a Theory of Instruction*, Harvard, Belknap Press.

CASSIRER, E. (1944) *An Essay on Man*, New Haven, CT, Yale University Press.

CASSIRER, E. (1955–8), *The Philosophy of Symbolic Forms*, 3 vols., New Haven, CT, Yale University Press.

COLERIDGE, S.T. (1975) *Biographia Literaria*, edited George Watson, London, Dent.

COLLINGWOOD, R.G. (1975) *The Principles of Art*, Oxford, Oxford University Press.

DEWEY, J. (1958) *Art as Experience*, New York, G.P. Putnam's Sons.

DONOGHUE, D. (1985) *The Arts Without Mystery*, London, BBC.

ELIOT, T.S. (1975) *Selected Prose*, edited Frank Kermode, London, Faber and Faber.

GRENE, M. (1966) *The Knower and the Known*, London, Faber and Faber.

GULBENKIAN FOUNDATION (1982) *The Arts in Schools*, London, Gulbenkian Foundation.

HARDING, D.W. (1937) 'The Role of the Onlooker', *Scrutiny*, **VI**, 3.

HARDING, D.W. (1962) 'Psychological Processes in the Reading of Fiction', *British Journal of Aesthetics*, **2**.

HARDING, D.W. (1982) *Experience into Words*, Cambridge, Cambridge University Press.

HARDING, R.E. (1948) *An Anatomy of Inspiration and an Essay on the Creative Mood*, 3rd. edn., Cambridge, Heffer.

HARGREAVES, D.J. (Ed.) (1989) *Children and the Arts*, Milton Keynes, Open University Press.

HILLMAN J. (1962) *Emotion*, London, Routledge and Kegan Paul.

HOSPERS, J. (1974) *Meaning and Truth in the Arts*, Chapel Hill, NC, University of North Carolina Press.

LANGER, S. (1953) *Feeling and Form*, London, Routledge and Kegan Paul.

LANGER, S. (1960) *Philosophy in a New Key*, Cambridge, MA, Harvard University Press.

LANGER, S. (1974) *Mind; an Essay on Human Feeling*, Baltimore, MD, Johns Hopkins University Press.

LAWRENCE, D.H. (1961) *Fantasia of the Unconscious*, London, Heinemann.

LEAVIS, F.R. (1976) *Thought, Words and Creativity*, London, Chatto and Windus.

LODGE, D. (1981) *Working with Structuralism*, London, Routledge and Kegan Paul.

MACLEISH, A. (1961) *Poetry and Experience*, London, Bodley Head.

MACMURRAY, J. (1953) *Reason and Emotion*, London, Faber and Faber.

MARGOLIS, J. (Ed.) (1978) *Philosophy Looks at the Arts*, revised edn., Philadelphia, Temple University Press.

MASLOW, A.H. (1968) *Towards a Psychology of Being*, 2nd. edn., New York, Van Nostrand Reinhold.

MAY, R. (1975) *The Courage to Create*, London, Collins.

MCKELLAR, P. (1957) *Imagination and Thinking*, London, Cohen and West.

POLANYI, M. (1958) *Personal Knowledge*, London, Routledge and Kegan Paul.

POLANYI, M. (1967) *The Tacit Dimension*, London, Routledge and Kegan Paul.

POLANYI, M. (1969) *Knowing and Being*, London, Routledge and Kegan Paul.

REID, L.A. (1961) *Ways of Knowledge and Experience*, London, Allen and Unwin.

REID, L.A. (1970) *Meaning in the Arts*, London, Allen and Unwin.

REID, L.A. (1986) *Ways of Understanding and Education*, London, Heinemann Educational Books.

RORTY, A.O. (Ed.) (1980) *Explaining Emotions*, Berkeley, CA, University of California Press.

ROSS, M. (1978) *The Creative Arts*, London, Heinemann Educational Books.

ROSS, M. (1975) *Arts and the Adolescent*, London, Evans Brothers.

ROSS, M. (1984) *The Aesthetic Imperative*, Oxford, Pergamon Press.

SALMON, P. (Ed.) (1973) *Coming to Know*, London, Routledge and Kegan Paul.

SCRUTON, R. (1983) *The Aesthetic Understanding*, London, Methuen.

SMITH, R.A. (Ed.) (1971) *Aesthetics and Problems of Education*, Champaign (Illinois), University of Illinois Press.

VYGOTSKY, L.S. (1962) *Thought and Language*, trans. Haufman and Vakar, Cambridge, MA, MIT Press.

WARNOCK, M. (1976) *Imagination*, London, Faber and Faber.

WITKIN, R. (1974) *The Intelligence of Feeling*, London, Heinemann Educational Books.

On English and the Teaching of Literature

ABBS, P. (1982) *English Within the Arts*, London, Hodder and Stoughton.

ALLEN, D. (1980) *English Teaching Since 1965*, London, Heinemann Educational Books.

ARNOLD, R. (1983) *Timely Voices: English Teaching in the 1980s*, Oxford, Oxford University Press.

BENTON, M. and FOX, G. (1985) *Teaching Literature: Nine to Fourteen*, Oxford, Oxford University Press.

BENTON, M. *et al.* (1988) *Young Readers Responding to Poems*, London, Routledge and Kegan Paul.

BENTON, P. (1986) *Pupil, Teacher, Poem*, London, Hodder and Stoughton.

CLEGG, A.B. (Ed.) (1964) *The Excitement of Writing*, London, Chatto and Windus Educational.

CLEGG, A.B. (Ed.) (1973) *Enjoying Writing*, London, Chatto and Windus Educational.

COOK, H.C. (1917) *The Play Way: an Essay in Educational Method*, London, Heinemann.

CREBER, J.W.P. (1965) *Sense and Sensitivity*, London, University of London Press.

DEMERS, P. (Ed.) (1986) *The Creating Word*, London, Macmillan.

DEPARTMENT OF EDUCATION AND SCIENCE (1975) *A Language for Life* (The Bullock Report), London, HMSO.

DEPARTMENT OF EDUCATION AND SCIENCE (1988) *Report of the Committee of Inquiry into the Teaching of the English Language* (The Kingman Report), London, HMSO.

DEPARTMENT OF EDUCATION AND SCIENCE (1989) *National Curriculum Proposals for English for Ages 5 to 16* (The Cox Report, Part Two), HMSO.

DIXON, J. (1975) *Growth Through English*, Oxford, Oxford University Press.

DRUCE, R. (1970) *The Eye of Innocence*, 2nd. edn., London, University of London Press.

FORD, B. (Ed.) (1970) *Young Writers, Young Readers*, London, Hutchinson.

GRIBBLE, J. (1985) *Literary Education: a Revaluation*, Cambridge, Cambridge University Press.

HARDY, B. (1973) 'Teaching Literature in the University', *English in Education*, **7**, 1.

HARRISON, B. (1982) *An Arts-Based Approach to English*, London, Hodder and Stoughton.

HOLBROOK, D. (1962) *English for Maturity*, Cambridge, Cambridge University Press.

HOLBROOK, D. (1967) *The Exploring Word*, Cambridge, Cambridge University Press.

HOLBROOK, D. (1979) *English for Meaning*, Windsor, NFER.

HOURD, M. (1949) *The Education of the Poetic Spirit*, London, Heinemann Educational Books.

HOURD, M. and COOPER, G. (1959) *Coming Into Their Own*, London, Heinemann.

HUGHES, T. (1969) *Poetry in the Making*, London, Faber and Faber.

INGLIS, F. (1969) *The Englishness of English Teaching*, London, Longmans.

KERMODE, F. (1975) *How We Read Novels*, Southampton, University of Southampton.

KNIGHT, R. (Ed.) (1989) *English in Practice: Literature at 'A' Level*, Edinburgh, Scottish Academic Press.

LANGDON, M. (1961) *Let the Children Write*, London, Longmans.

LEAVIS, F.R. (1975) *The Living Principle*, London, Chatto and Windus.

LEE, V.J. (1986) *English Literature in Schools*, Milton Keynes, Open University Press.

MARSH, G. (1988) *Teaching Through Poetry: Writing and the Drafting Process*, London, Hodder and Stoughton.

MARSHALL, S. (1963) *An Experiment in Education*, Cambridge, Cambridge University Press.

MATHIESON, M. (1975) *The Preachers of Culture*, London, Allen and Unwin.

PROTHEROUGH, R. (1983) *Developing Responses to Fiction*, Milton Keynes, Open University Press.

ROBINSON, I. (1973) *The Survival of English*, Cambridge, Cambridge University Press.

ROSENBLATT, L. (1970) *Literature as Exploration*, London, Heinemann Educational Books.

SAMPSON, G. (1975) *English for the English*, Cambridge, Cambridge University Press.

SCHAYER, D. (1972) *The Teaching of English in Schools 1900–1970*, London, Routledge and Kegan Paul.

SCHIFF, H. (Ed.) (1977) *Contemporary Approaches to English Studies*, London, Heinemann Educational Books.

WHITEHEAD, F. (1968) *The Disappearing Dais*, London, Chatto and Windus.

Index

Index

mind 5, 9, 71, 73, 88
  see also psyche
models, scientific 12, 16n
monologue 120, 128
Mozart, Wolfgang Amadeus 19
music 41–2, 47n, 50, 110, 130n
  see also arts
myth 4, 5, 111

Nabokov, Vladimir 90
narration, oral 41–2, 46, 110, 116, 119
narrative 5, 24, 30, 31, 96, 97, 127, 132,
  139, 143–4, 148
  modes of 45
National Curriculum, The xii
natural language 125
neuropsychology 60, 65n
Newsom Report viii

O'Brien, V. 120
objectivity/subjectivity 3, 7–15, 30, 33,
  57, 60–1, 70–1, 105, 108
Operative Response 140
oral projection of poetry 114–6, 119–29
'organic form' 80–1

painting 49, 62, 65–6n, 73, 78–9, 111
  see also arts
parable-art 13, 58
parody 119–20
Pavlov, I. 60
perception 76–80, 86, 106, 121, 140
percepts/recollects *see* images, sensory
Perceptual Response 140
performance *see* drama, presentational
  form, aesthetic field
personality 59, 69–71, 137–8
  integration of 19, 59–61, 88
personal writing 95–6
phantasy 13
Picasso, Pablo 65n
play, art as 36
poetic image, the 21–2
poetic memory 21
poetry 119–29
  and tradition 38–40
  lyric 24, 30–1, 122
  origin of word 20
  poetry making 18–25, 49, 57–9, 80,
    113–7, 117–8n
  'puzzle interest' xvi, 36, 121
points-of-view, the novel 31, 32n
Polanyi, Michael 61, 62
'pollyanalytics' (Lawrence) 61

Pope, Alexander 55
'post-language' symbolization 55–6
post-structuralism *see* structuralism
Pound, Ezra 80
prejudice 131
presenting *see* aesthetic field,
  presentational form
presentational form 105, 107, 109–17,
  142, 149
'primitive' painting 35–6
prophecy, art as xvii–xviii
propositional thinking 65n, 69
prosody 121
psyche, 3, 5–7, 10, 11, 17, 38
psychiatry 9
psychology 9, 132
psychopathology 59
psychotherapy 11, 59
  activity-method 88–9

rationalism 4, 7, 10–11, 15–16n, 52, 60,
  61, 69, 73, 76–8
Read, Herbert 80
reading xvii, 32, 45, 62, 63, 71, 101,
  107–9, 112, 120–2, 135, 139, 149
  sensuous experience of 21, 25, 107,
    117, 139, 149
  psychology of 140–1
  'writerly' reading 109
realization, defined 20
reason, reasoning *see* rationalism
recitation 120, 129
recollection (of experience) 18, 19–22,
  51–3, 96–7
  of memory images in poetry 22–30,
    32, 85–6
  see also memory
recollects/percepts *see* images, sensory
Reed, Henry 128
responding *see* aesthetic field
rhyme 4, 64, 121
Richards, I.A. 13–14
role-play 78, 145
  see also drama
Romantic movement 137
Rorschach tests 11
Rose Theatre 132
Rousseau, Jean-Jacques 73
Ryle, Gilbert 76–7

Sampson, George ix, xiv
Saussure, Ferdinand de 51